SONOMA
PICNIC

A California Wine Country
Travel Companion

SONOMA PICNIC

A California Wine Country Travel Companion

by
Jack Burton

BORED FEET PRESS
Mendocino, California
2000

© 1999 by Jack Burton
First Edition, January 2000
Printed in Canada on recycled paper

Cover and book design by Elizabeth Petersen
Cover illustration and maps by Marsha Mello
Edited by Donna Bettencourt & Bob Lorentzen
Composition by Petersen Graphics, Fort Bragg, CA

Published by Bored Feet Press
Post Office Box 1832
Mendocino, California 95460
707-964-6629 · 888-336-6199
Fax: 707-964-5953
E-mail: boredfeet@mcn.org
Web: www.sonomapicnic.com
       www.boredfeet.com (coming Spring 2000)

Library of Congress Cataloging-in-Publication Data

Burton, Jack, 1951–
    Sonoma picnic : a California wine country travel companion : picnic sources, menus & recipes, great picnic spots, favorite wineries, stories & diversions / Jack Burton.— 1st ed.
      p. cm.
    Includes bibliographical references and index.
    ISBN 0-939431-22-X
    1. Picnicking. 2. Menus. 3. Sonoma County (Calif.)—Guidebooks. I. Title.

TX823 .B89 1999
917.94'180453—dc21   99-051721

ISBN 0-939431-22-X
10 9 8 7 6 5 4 3 2 1

This book is dedicated
to the memory of
T-Bud,
our favorite winery cat.

"To beg silently
is bliss."

■ Acknowledgments

First and foremost, I wish to thank my wife and picnic partner, Janette.

Credit is due my sister, Arlyne Burton, for the many hours of deciphering my handwritten manuscript, for the typing, and for bringing form to this book.

Thanks to Cathleen Francisco for saying, "What a good idea, write that book!"

"¡Grazie mille!" to Cynthia DeMartini and Gloria French for proofreading, neighbors Ron and MaryAnn for reading the rough new work, and to everyone at Preston Vineyards.

With deep appreciation I acknowledge the support and enthusiasm of the Sterling family, their chef Mark Malicki, and all my co-workers at Iron Horse Vineyards.

Special thanks to everyone who took time to provide information, to Murphy Business Services of Healdsburg, and to all the folks at Bored Feet Press.

■ Photo Credits

Pages 5, 75: Preston Vineyards
Pages 14, 53, 92, 141: Liz Petersen
Pages 26, 29: Jack Burton
Page 28: (top) Bellwether Farms, (bottom) Redwood Hill Dairy
Page 30: Bodega Goat Cheese
Page 73: Armida Winery
Page 79: Forrest Tanser

■ Preface

Having been picnic aficionados for many years, we didn't waste time after our move to this celebrated wine country picking up on the pleasure of packing a meal and getting together with good friends to head for the source of our favorite wines.

We enjoy a simple Mediterranean approach to our picnic meals: bread from the baker, local cheese, and something seasonal from the farmer's garden. After an hour's shopping, coffee and chatter with the shopkeepers, a stop at the deli, we're ready to head out into the countryside with a harmonious wine pairing in mind. We take along a small cutting board, a little cook's knife and a few staples so we can elaborate on our purchases.

An extra element of enjoyment pervades dining out amongst the vines or along the byways. Following the ancient Mediterranean custom, we like to pour a little splash of wine out onto the ground in salute to the gods and winemakers. Won't you join us in the circle from earth and grape to picnic table and glass?

Welcome!
Jack and Janette Burton

Contents

1
Welcome to the Neighborhood

"Caw, caw, caw!" It's the morning call of resident crows, hashing over the day's plans. "Where shall we eat? Where shall we eat?" says the ravenous chorus.

"The vineyards," says one to the others. "There's still plenty of sweet dry fruit, and those biped groundlings haven't yet finished with their pruning."

"Caw, caw, indeed," injects another. "What about the parking lot at the donut shop? The grounded ones are famously careless with their morning treats, and there are no seagulls in from the coast to steal our crumbs." So goes the conversation in the fir tree.

I am making a pot of green tea as the sun rises through a mist veil. An elastic fog follows the Russian River's snaking path around Fitch Mountain, past our town of Healdsburg, then down through the redwoods to the sea.

I hear more shrill squawking from the backyard. The bluejays have started their daily argument and the scolding of the local cats. It will go on for them like this for most of the day.

"Where have the crows gone for their breakfast?" comes a little voice out of a pile of blankets in the bedroom.

"The crows have decided it's bugs for breakfast! I can see them out in the ballfield behind the middle school, and the brown towhees are peeping for their seeds in the garden."

"Yum," says my wife, cozy on our day off. "Bring me some tea, then let's plan a picnic!"

This book tells how to plan your own Sonoma picnic: how to plan your picnic menu and find your picnic supplies at our wonderful local food shops and outlets. We suggest convenient recipes and where you might picnic all over Sonoma County's gorgeous countryside. The book also serves as a practical tour guide to wineries, restaurants and other diversions you might enjoy in the area.

The book organizes this neighborhood, referred to as the West County, into general areas which roughly correspond to the wine-growing regions of Dry Creek Valley, Alexander Valley and the town of Healdsburg, the Russian River and Green Valley appellations, and the coastal area south to Tomales Bay and north to Gualala. We include information

Sonoma and neighboring counties.

on the Sonoma Valley (East County) in a special chapter since it is separated by both geography and history from the Healdsburg neighborhood and our West County areas of interest.

Whatever your mode of transportation, a day's sojourn will reward you with the opportunity to enjoy vineyards, lakeshore, riverfront, redwood forests, friendly small towns or Pacific Coast. Though you may actually be staying in Cloverdale, Geyserville, Monte Rio or on the coast, we have chosen Healdsburg as the focal point and starting place for trips and adventures. The town of Healdsburg enjoys a fortunate location near the center of the county in that it is situated on the major north/south Highway 101 and the banks of the Russian River. Everything you need for the day's picnic is readily available within a pleasant four-block walk.

■ About the Weather and Seasons

In the interest of best planning and enjoying your visit to Sonoma County, we'll start with a summary of the weather and seasons. For the most part, our area has a moderate, marine-influenced climate with extremes ranging from the often cool and foggy coast to the northern Alexander Valley at Cloverdale where it can be very hot and dry in the summer. You may experience the exceptional January day at Bodega Head whale-watching in your shirt sleeves, or the cold mid-September rain that stalls the grape harvest and ruins the best laid plans of patio chefs. Mostly, though, it is quite temperate.

Considering the fickle moods of Mother Nature, we suggest a sweater, windbreaker and sunscreen in our dry season, April through October. Our wet or winter season runs from November through March, and heavier clothing, rain gear and sunscreen are recommended.

For up-to-date weather, visit our award-winning local newspaper, the Santa Rosa Press Democrat, on the World Wide Web at www.pressdemo.com, or call Sonoma County Airport Automated Weather Observation Station at 707-573-8393.

Your local librarian can help you get online if you are not already plugged in at home or at work. Also check out the travel section at your library or your local book store for more Sonoma County information.

■ Where to Stay

All the points of interest discussed in this book are within easy driving distance of anywhere in Sonoma, Marin and San Francisco counties. If our vine country and its delicious wines are what you fancy, the Healdsburg area offers the ideal place to stay. If your interests are more coastal, then your best choice may be Jenner, Bodega Bay, Timber Cove, Sea Ranch/Gualala, Occidental, or the Point Reyes/Tomales Bay area. Then again, you can always split the difference with cozy river digs from Forestville to Monte Rio. Don't overlook the option of camping in the redwoods, on the Russian River, at the coast, or at Lake Sonoma. Whatever your choice, it's best to call ahead for reservations, particularly in summer when everything from your cousin Marty's futon to our finest hostelry can be booked 100%.

You'll find a list of lodgings, organized by area, in **Appendix B: Where to Stay**. For Sonoma Valley lodging, refer to **Chapter 8**. If you're reading this from outside of Sonoma County or northern California, you might want to refer to **Appendix A: Getting Here/Mode of Travel**. For trip planning, you may also find some useful information on the San Francisco Bay Area and our neighboring counties in **Chapter 10: Heading In/Heading Out**.

■ Camping

What is camping but an extended picnic combined with slumber in the great outdoors? Sonoma County abounds with great attractive and spacious campgrounds and the mild climate entices campers throughout the long season. Even the dead of winter offers pleasant camping if you're prepared, particularly along the coast where the ocean moderates the cool winter nightime temperatures. In summer, especially on weekends, you'll probably need a reservation. For a list of the park choices and how to contact them, see Campgrounds in **Appendix B**. For private campgrounds in the area, consult the Yellow Pages.

2
The Traveling Picnicker

From wherever you wake up here in Sonoma County, a pleasant hour of shopping will reward you with a tasty and economical prelude to the day's travels. This chapter will introduce you to the food producers, farmers, markets and grocers of our neighborhood who will assist you in assembling a satisfying picnic lunch or dinner. Then we suggest some favorite wineries where you can enjoy your meal with the fruit of the vintner's labor, or pick up a bottle and head for the beach.

■ Picnic Paraphernalia

Gear for the successful picnic tourist can be as simple as a Swiss Army knife, tin cups and plates. You can also go to the extreme: full-dress basket, cooler, Coleman stove, folding chairs and table kit that old Uncle Louie hauls around in the RV. We must admit we are almost as well prepared as Louie, but we normally choose the middle ground and travel fairly light.

Here are the Basics:

basket or day pack

small tablecloth and/or picnic blanket

luncheon-size plates (enamel-ware is nice)

larger plate or platter for serving

Tupperware-type bowl, large enough to toss four salads, with a good sealing lid

forks, spoons, butter knife

sturdy nesting glasses

2 tea or dish towels to wrap the glasses

corkscrew

simple, old-fashioned can opener

*small, all-purpose camp or cook's knife with
blade guard*

small, wood cutting board, 5" x 8" is all you need

cloth or paper napkins

oyster knife (optional)

small cooler (allows you an expanded menu)

We also carry the following easily-transportable staples to prepare the picnic recipe items and to season prepared and deli-purchased foods:

small container of coarse salt

small pepper mill with black peppercorns

small jar of a favorite mustard

8-ounce bottle of extra-virgin olive oil

small, well-sealed bottle of wine vinegar

bulb of fresh garlic

lemon or lime

◆

Our picnic kit has been accumulating for years, but if you want to toss one together on the spur of the moment, we suggest a trip to one of our local thrift stores. Or, we can recommend a visit to one of our premier picnic outfitters:

> **Robinson & Co.**
> 108 Matheson Street
> On the Healdsburg Plaza
> 707-433-7116

Jimtown Store
6706 State Highway 128
In the Alexander Valley
707-433-1212

Sign of the Bear
435 First Street West
Sonoma, CA 95476
707-996-3722

◆

You might also visit our website at www.sonomapicnic.com. It's the wine country online.

■ Bicycle Touring

Cycling offers a great way to see the wine country! Here are some rental opportunities, repair shops and tour companies that will help make your visit safe and fun. Do keep in mind that bike travel and extensive wine tasting are not a very good combination, as appealing as the idea might be.

HEALDSBURG

Getaway Wine Country Bicycle Tours and Rental
800-499-2453

Spoke Folk Cyclery
249 Center Street
707-433-7171
Rentals, repairs and parts.

Event Note: The month of July features the Healdsburg Harvest Century Bicycle Tour. Tour maps and information are available at the Healdsburg Chamber of Commerce, 707-433-6935.

CLOVERDALE

Cloverdale Cyclery
125 N. Cloverdale Boulevard
707-894-2841
Rentals, repairs and parts.

POINT REYES STATION

Building Supply
11280 State Route 1
415-663-1737
Rentals.

OLEMA

Trailhead Rental
415-663-1958
Rentals and camping supplies.

NEAR SONOMA

If you're going to the Sonoma Valley, bicycle touring is an excellent way to see that area, which has more designated bike paths than the rest of Sonoma County. For bicycle travel and services there, contact the following businesses:

Goodtime Bicycle Company
18503 Sonoma Highway, Sonoma
707-938-0453
Rentals, sales, repairs, helpful information.

Bikeman Bicycle Touring and Rentals
18503 State Highway 12, Sonoma
1-888-525-0453
www.bikemantours.com

Bikeman does it all, Sonoma Valley bicycle excursions for as few as two, or more. These good folks provide the bikes, tailor the ride, and set up the lunch.

Give them a call and skip the shopping for your wine country picnic.

> **Sonoma Valley Cyclery**
> 20093 Broadway, Sonoma
> 707-935-3377
> *Sales, repairs.*

■ Motorcycle Touring

Sonoma County's winding back roads offer a motorcyclist's dream come true, but only if you're used to that kind of two wheeling. Many bikers tour the county regularly, coming from far and wide. Remember that California has a mandatory helmet law for both driver and rider. If you'd like to rent a motorcycle for your Sonoma County tour, see the listings in **Appendix A.**

3
Shopping for Your Picnic

The picnic tourist in Sonoma County is blessed with endless potential for creative economical meals based on fresh, locally grown and prepared foods. We will introduce you to the producers and their products. Then we'll detail the retail sources where you can easily put your afternoon feast together.

Gathered here from far and wide with backgrounds as varied as the products they provide, northern California's farmers, bakers, vintners and cheese makers share the luck of soil and climate. Theirs is a fortune of time and place, of common view, and tables' grace.

THE FOODS

■ Bread and Bakers

Good bread is the foundation upon which a great Sonoma picnic is built. The staff of life has been in the western world the essential ingredient for the traveler's menu for a long, long time. It is our good fortune to be able to introduce you to the following artisans.

Downtown Bakery and Creamery
308-A Center Street
Healdsburg
707-431-2719
First class and not to be missed. The Downtown Bakery is the place for morning coffee and pastries,

*breads, and all manner of straightforward goodness
from the ovens. Owner Kathleen Stewart also makes
the County's best ice cream and fresh seasonal sorbet.*

Forno at Preston Vineyards
9282 W. Dry Creek Road
Healdsburg
707-433-3372

*This is just the first
mention in our book
about Preston Vine-
yards. Not only is it our
favorite picnic spot, but
also now the site of a new,
wood-fired bread oven.
Owner Lou Preston con-
tinues to amaze and
delight us with some of*

Stubs—Preston Vineyards

*the best rustic loaves we have ever eaten. Call ahead to
see what's available. Bread Hotline: 707-433-4720.*

Della Fattoria
707-762-1722

*In a brick wood-fired oven on the family farm,
Cathleen, Ed and Aaron Webber hearth-bake wonderful bread in the Italian style. Lucky for us, they deliver
regularly to Oakville Grocery in Healdsburg. Try
some!*

Village Bakery
7225 Healdsburg Avenue
Sebastopol
707-829-8101

*Look for Brigitta Schofield's delicious loaves at
Ansteads or Big John's Markets in Healdsburg, Speer's
Market in Forestville, Bartlett's General Store in
Monte Rio, or Gonnella's in Occidental. Visit the
Bakery—it's just down Highway 116 in Sebastopol.*

Wild Flour Bakers

140 Bohemian Highway
Freestone
707-874-2938

West County hot-out-of-the-wood-fired-oven. Coffees, breakfast pastry and excellent breads. A great place to stop on your way to or from the coast!

Artisan Bakers

750 West Napa
Sonoma
707-939-1765

These folks do a great job. We recommend their Italian Country Walnut and Pugliese loaves for sandwiches or for simply dipping in good olive oil. Available at Oakville Grocery in Healdsburg and Speer's Market in Forestville, or visit the bakery.

■ Cheese Makers

Northern California is home to literally herds of dairy goats, cows and sheep. Winter rains refresh miles of rolling coastal grasslands and snug valleys. The following is a brief introduction to some of our favorite cheese makers and their products. Most of these cheeses are available at several locations.

Bellwether Farms

707-778-0774

Cheese maker Cindy Callahan produces a variety of extraordinary cheeses from both Jersey cow and sheep milk. Keep your eye out for these favorites at Oakville Grocery in Healdsburg or Tomales Bay Foods in Point Reyes Station:

Toscano — aged sheep-milk cheese

Caciotta — a young Toscano

Pepato — aged Toscano with black peppercorns

San Andreas — semi-soft sheep-milk cheese

Ricotta — fresh sheep-milk cheese

Part of the Crew at Bellwether Farms

Carmody — a buttery, Jersey cow-milk cheese, aged four to six weeks

Crescenza — a beautifully rich and tart young cheese in the Italian style of Lombardy

Laura Chenel Chevre
707-996-4477
Conveniently packaged for picnics and available at most grocers, this mild goat-milk cheese is great with olive salad on a baguette.

Redwood Hill Farm
707-823-8250
Two hundred and fifty dairy goats, and each one has a name. Happy herds make for great cheese! We really like their small, French-style Crottin, perfect for a picnic for two. They also make yogurt, fresh chevre, feta, and a delicious camellia, a camembert-style

Redwood Hill Farm Saanen bucks. "The Guys" (l-r): Chojuro, Katsui, Prime Rate and Prototype.

mold-ripened cheese. Available at Ansteads Market and Oakville Grocery in Healdsburg, Food for Humans in Guerneville, and Tomales Bay Foods in Point Reyes Station.

Joe Matos Cheese
3669 Llano Road
Santa Rosa
707-584-5283

The Matos family are true farmstead producers. Look for their wonderful St. Jorge aged Holstein cow-milk cheese at Oakville Grocery in Healdsburg, Tomales Bay Foods in Point Reyes Station, or visit the farm just east of Sebastopol off Highway 12.

New additon to Joe Matos Dairy.

Cypress Grove
707-839-3168

From up in Humboldt County comes goat-milk cheese that will take you back to France. These folks do a terrific job with both fresh and ripened cheeses; we really enjoy their Humboldt Fog.

Look for Cypress Grove products at Oakville Grocery in Healdsburg, or Tomales Bay Foods in Point Reyes Station.

Bodega Goat Cheese
P.O. Box 223
Bodega, CA 94922
707-876-3483

These wonderful fresh and aged Peruvian-style country cheeses are available at Fiesta Market and Food for Thought in Sebastopol, the Valley Ford Market, or at the family shop, the Gourmet Goat in Bodega. We particularly enjoy picking up a small container of queso crema to eat with local strawberries amidst fields of wildflowers at Bodega Head.

*Mulberry &
Blueberry
—two of the
resi-dents at
Bodega
Goat Cheese*

Marin French Cheese Company
7500 Redhill Road
Petaluma
707-762-6001
Look for conveniently packaged and delicious Rouge et Noir brand camembert, brie, breakfast cheese and tangy schloss cheese. Available at most grocers or visit the factory on the way to Point Reyes.

Cowgirl Creamery at Tomales Bay Foods
80 Fourth at B Street
Point Reyes Station
415-663-9335
Chef Peggy Smith and cheese maker Sue Conley have created simply the most tasteful, one-stop delicious, picnic shopping venue around! The Creamery produces wonderful fresh chevre, cottage cheese, creme fraîche, quark and seasonally-flavored ice creams. Under one roof, the owners not only produce, but have assembled, the finest selection of locally produced cheeses to be found anywhere. Don't miss Peggy's superb prepared foods, organic produce, and some thoughtful wine choices.

Vella Cheese Company of Sonoma
315 Second Street East
P.O. Box 191
Sonoma
1-800-848-0505
www.vellacheese.com
Purveyors of fine handmade cheese since 1931.

Look for Bear Flag brand cheese at most local grocers and delis. We are particularly fond of their asiago and special select dry Monterey jack.

When visiting over in Sonoma, stop in to see the various cheeses being made. Informal tours start at 12:30 p.m. Monday through Thursday.

Clover-Stornetta Farms
707-778-8448

All kinds of dairy products fresh, wholesome, and available everywhere.

Old-Time Religion

I have for some time now sensed the return of some ancient religious traditions among everyday working folks, a deep stirring of archaic cult-memory welling up out of a distant past.

I'm talking about cows. Have you noticed a subtle increase in the number of vehicles on the road with those fuzzy, faux-cow seat covers? What about the cow cardigan sweaters, and all manner of cow-kitsch gizmos, greeting cards and gift items? My wife Janette says, "Yes, dear, there goes another minivan with those cow seat covers, but it doesn't mean anything, really."

"What about all the milk mustaches?" I ask. "What about 'Got Milk?' You can't escape those cute little Got Milk Kids."

Living here in Sonoma County, home to Clover-Stornetta Farms Dairy and their omnipresent spokes ruminant, Clo the Cow, only reinforced my suspicions. "You can't explain away Clo the Cow. Look around. She's doing wacky things on billboards all over the place," I argued calmly. I'm prone to conspiracy theories; the sixties hit me hard that way. My wife pretends not to notice. While out shopping the other day, I spotted a cow-painted straightback chair with a bright pink wooden udder slung under the seat. "Cute," she says. "Duh," like oblivious, I'm thinking.

I began to get the bigger picture on the day we chanced upon the lovely little town of Point Reyes

Station, just south of the Sonoma County line in Marin County. This is prime dairy country at the south end of Tomales Bay with sheep, goats, cows and rolling green coastal rangeland for as far as the eye can see.

"Neo-cowvanism!" It hit me. "Earth Mother, Cult of the Teat," I blurted out to Janette.

We stopped in the Bovine Bakery, where we encountered the mellow local supplicants indulging in the sacred latté.

"Nothing dark about this Cowvanist Culture but the roast on their coffee beans," she replied sagely.

We wandered out into a sweet wind off the Bay. I felt myself giving in to the smell of newly mown hay in the pastures, the light on the hillsides. We wandered down the main drag past the Western Saloon. There two horses were tied to the old-fashioned hitching posts outside the bar. Somewhere up the street a loudspeaker bawled out an unmistakable and prolonged, "M . . . m . . . mooo . . ." Scout's honor, this town has forsaken the time-honored Cold War tradition of the eerie siren-wail at noon for the "m . . . m . . . mooo . . ." over a loudspeaker.

"Heiferites," I muttered to Janette, ancient mystique of Cow Goddess devotion.

This little train of thought all came together for me when we found ourselves at the Cowgirl Creamery in Tomales Bay Foods at the corner of Fourth and B Streets. I was blown away, slack-jawed before an altar of local cheeses: sheep-milk, goat-milk, cow-milk! Cheeses aged and young, cottage cheese fresh as a calf's lunch of daisies, cheeses to fall in love over, sweet as little spring lambs, cheeses, tart like an afternoon's tryst, and cheeses, ripe and lusty like big red wines.

"Have mercy!" I exclaimed, nearly blinded by my enlightenment. "Well, well," said my wife, with a poke in the ribs, "Mother works in mysterious ways!"

―――

■ Farm-Fresh Produce

A small Green Revelation is occurring in our neighborhood. As distinct from the Green Revolution, this Green Revelation has little to do with the ingenious new genetically-engineered crops and livestock usually associated with questionable government subsidies and giant agribusiness. It has its roots in the patient collecting and cultivation of near-forgotten varieties of truck crops, the preservation of Grandpa's pickle recipe, and a realization that the best route for the cradle to grave journey may not necessarily involve all the convenient bypasses and express lanes of this modern life. Happily our neighborhood is home to a dedicated bunch of families who have chosen to remain on or move back to the land and provide us with the bounty of the seasons.

For the best source of farm and produce information, we recommend you pick up a copy of the *Sonoma County Farm Trails Map and Guide*, available free at local chamber of commerce offices and visitor's centers throughout Sonoma County. You can also write for a copy. Please enclose 77 cents postage.

Sonoma County Farm Trails
PO Box 6032
Santa Rosa, CA 95406
1-800-207-9464
www.farmtrails.org

You may also want to write or call the following outstanding non-profit organization for a copy of the *Select Sonoma* magazine. It includes an excellent list of Sonoma-grown and Sonoma-made products, plus farm and farmers market information.

Select Sonoma County
5000 Roberts Lake Road, Suite A
Rohnert Park, CA 94928
707-586-2233
www.sonomagrown.com

■ Farmers Markets

The farmers markets in our area provide your best source of local seasonal produce, flowers, honey, and farm-crafted products. The market season is generally May through November. We eagerly await the first market days of spring for fresh flowers or the early salad mixes and greens. Market days are also pleasant social occasions with pre-market coffees and streetside chit-chat: "Who's got what?" "Is there any asparagus yet?" "Peaches next week!" A good deal of strategy is in play as the shoppers try to look casual while positioning themselves for the critical first purchases when market opens at the sound of the bell. You have to be ready for the scarce half dozen bunches of those tiny golden beets or tri-color radishes. The friendly competition can be fierce with rival chefs and restauranteurs imagining the day's specials as they edge their way towards a particularly choice display of Mother Earth's fleeting treasures. Market days allow us to savor the scenic backroads of life and the flavors of foods true to the time and place.

Healdsburg Farmers Market

This colorful gathering of area farmers offers a good place to start your Saturdays from May through November, 9 a.m. to noon, downtown in West Plaza Park. The Market also happens at the Vintage Plaza Antiques parking lot at the corner of Healdsburg Avenue and Mill Street on Tuesdays, June through October, 4 p.m. to 6:30 p.m. Say hello to our friends, and enjoy the best of the season.

Point Reyes Station Saturday Farmers Market at Toby's Feed Barn

11250 Highway 1 (Main Street)
Point Reyes Station
415-663-1223
Join the good folks of West Marin County every Saturday, mid-April through mid-October, 9 a.m. until noon.

You might also want to visit one of the following markets slightly out of our neighborhood but within an easy drive:

Railroad Square Farm Market

On the west side of Highway 101 at the corner of Wilson and 4th Street in downtown Santa Rosa. Wednesdays, June through October, 9:30 a.m. to 12:30 p.m.

Santa Rosa Original Farm Market

Held year round on Wednesdays and Saturdays, 8:30 a.m. until noon (until 11 a.m. on rainy days), in the parking lot of the Veteran's Building, north side of Highway 12 at Maple Street just south of downtown Santa Rosa.

Sebastopol Farm Market

West County fresh foods every Sunday, 10 a.m. until 1:30 p.m. in the downtown plaza off McKinley Street in Sebastopol just across the street from Food for Thought.

Sonoma Valley Farm Market

Friday market year round at Arnold Field in Depot Park, 9 a.m. until noon, one block and a little bit north of the Sonoma Plaza, downtown Sonoma. From April through October a Tuesday evening market also occurs on the Sonoma Plaza from 5:30 p.m. until dusk.

◆

Most grocery stores, and particularly the better delis, now work more with local farmers and organic suppliers. **Oakville Grocery** and **Ansteads Market** in Healdsburg, **Food for Humans** in Guerneville, and **Tomales Bay Foods** in Point Reyes Station exemplify this approach to produce marketing.

■ Olives and Olive Oil

Olive trees came to Sonoma County with some of the first Spanish settlers in the 1830s. Later, Italian families brought more trees to cure the fruits and grace their tables with the indispensable oil of Mediterranean cooking.

Lately, along with the resurgent interest in all things culinary, winemakers and growers are planting more and more olive trees and producing their own estate-bottled extra-virgin olive oils. So take advantage of this revival and try a local bottle. Pour a bit of your favorite oil on a plate, dip your fresh bread or vegetable, take a bite and experience the local blend of tastes.

For more information and a good selection, visit or call our friends at:

> **Olive Press**
> 14301 Arnold Drive
> Glen Ellen
> 707-939-8900

For cured olives, we recommend imported varieties, and the best selection in the West County is at **Oakville Grocery** in Healdsburg.

■ Seafood

Your picnic menus can easily include the bountiful fruits of the nearby Pacific Ocean, among the great flavor sensations of Sonoma County. Try local smoked salmon and an Alexander Valley Sauvignon Blanc, or a sweet bay shrimp salad sandwich with a crisp Green Valley Chardonnay. You have vastly expanded possibilities with cured, smoked and fully cooked seafoods.

CURED, SMOKED AND FULLY COOKED SEAFOOD

Fish Dock Seafood Market and Deli
1005 Vine
Healdsburg
2 blocks west of the Plaza
707-433-0515
Fresh from Bodega Bay—all your picnic seafood, plus great sandwiches, salads and fish and chips.

Ducktrap River Fish Farm
P.O. Box 257
Sonoma
800-434-8727
Smoked Atlantic salmon, smoked mussels and tasty smoked whitefish paté. Available at Oakville Grocery in Healdsburg.

Crab Pot
1750 Highway 1
Bodega Bay
707-875-9970
Just a little hole in the wall, but well worth a look-see! Say hello to Billie, and pick up great local smoked fish and fresh crab in season.

Tides Wharf Fish Market
835 Highway 1
Bodega Bay
707-875-3554
Freshly cooked crab in season, smoked salmon, ready-to-peel-and-eat shrimp and plenty of choices for the picnic, plus sandwiches, a bar and restaurant.

OYSTERS

Hog Island Oyster Company

Located on Tomales Bay at the town of Marshall, nine miles north of Point Reyes Station

415-663-9218

If you like oysters, this is one stop you should make. We like to plan a day at the beach around an oyster feast, and there's no better spot than the picnic grounds at Hog Island for that! The place is at its funky best on a sunny day. We call ahead for a weather report and to make sure they are open and have oysters available. Sweetwater, Atlantic, Kumamoto or European oysters—we eat them by the dozen. They also have Manila clams and Mediterranean mussels.

First we make a stop at Iron Horse Vineyards for our oyster beverage of choice, their Classic Vintage Brut. Another stop is the Marshall Store, one-half mile south of Hog Island, for soda crackers and a bottle from the store's world-class selection of hot sauces. You might also get some briquettes if you like barbecued oysters, clams or mussels. Hog Island provides the Weber grills.

Hog Island provides tables, oysterman's gloves, an oyster knife and Weber grills—you're free to shuck till your wrist goes numb. Play with the resident cats, work on your tan, waltz your sweetheart down to the bayshore and dance a fox trot in the mud . . . it's that kind of place—inspiring!

◆

The area has two other choices for fresh shellfish:

Tomales Bay Oyster Company

P.O. Box 296

Point Reyes Station

415-663-1242

Located on Highway 1 just south of the town of Marshall

Johnson Oyster Company
P.O. Box 69
Inverness
415-669-1149

Located in the Point Reyes National Seashore off Sir Francis Drake Blvd. Look for the sign and turn off as you follow the road out to the lighthouse.

CANNED FISH AND SHELLFISH

With the profusion of beautiful new cookbooks on the market, it is rare to find any mention of the old working-class picnic standards like sardines in mustard sauce, kippered snacks, pickled herring or smoked tiny oysters and clams. Down but not out, King Oscar still shares shelf space with the Tiny Tots Brisling Sardine and the Spirit of Norway products. For me, these all make great handy picnic treats. I fondly remember my Dad's "fisherman's lunch" of sardines on soda crackers with an ice-cold beer.

■ Picnic Meats and Poultry

This section offers a note on food safety. *Sonoma Picnic* does not address any serious cooking or barbecuing. The guide is meant to encourage the casual traveler to patronize our fine local delis, farm markets and grocers. When it comes to meat or poultry items for your menus, we suggest you purchase fully cooked products, and if you buy them hot (rotisserie chicken, fried chicken or ribs), eat them hot and promptly. If you purchase fully cooked cold sausages, roast chicken or chicken salads, keep them cold and eat them cold. Of course you may re-heat precooked and chilled meats, fish or poultry over a twig fire (see page 65) or charcoal. Avoid the hazard of

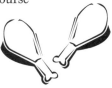

purchasing that gorgeous, crisp, rotisserie chicken, then making a couple of wine-tasting stops before you eat it. Purchase hot foods with a specific picnic stop in mind and get right to the business of lunch.

While there's nothing wrong with a good old-fashioned Chicago hot dog or kielbasa to accompany your meal, we now have some other delicious and fully cooked sausages to choose from. We recommend you try the conveniently packaged products produced right here in northern California:

Bruce Aidell's Suasage Company of San Leandro

Evergood Sausage Company of San Francisco

Gerhard's Napa Valley Sausages of Napa

Montibella Sausage Company of Orinda

Schwarz Sausage Company of San Francisco

◆

Cured and dried meats are a good choice for your picnic and hiking menus. I defer to the helpful staff at any of our fine deli counters to help you choose from the multitude of imported and local products that make for delicious sandwiches and accompaniments.

THE SHOPS

■ Healdsburg Shopping

Downtown Bakery and Creamery
308-A Center Street, on the Plaza
707-431-2719
Morning coffee and pastries, breads and picnic tarts, cake, cookies and fresh fruit compote. Best homemade ice cream.

Oakville Grocery
124 Matheson
707-433-3200
One-stop deluxe!

Healdsburg Natural Foods
325 Center Street
707-433-1060
Organic foods, health, diet and body care.

Fish Dock Fresh Seafood Market and Deli
1005 Vine Street
One block west of the Plaza
707-433-0515
First-rate local cracked crabs in season.

Ansteads Market
102 Healdsburg Avenue
707-431-0530
One-stop organic, and the best herb and garlic roast free-range chicken in the County. Well worth the walk four blocks south of the Plaza.

Healdsburg Farmers Market
707-433-6935

Saturdays: May through November, from 9 a.m. to noon, in West Plaza Park. Tuesdays: June through October, from 4 p.m. to 6:30 p.m., at the Vintage Plaza Antiques parking lot, corner of Healdsburg Avenue and Mill Street. The best local growers!

Jimtown Store in the Alexander Valley
6706 State Highway 128
707-433-1212

First class take-away foods and homemade picnic condiments. A couple of miles north and east of town, but worth a trip.

■ Sebastopol Shopping

Located eight miles west of Santa Rosa at the junction of Highway 12 and Highway 116, Sebastopol lies slightly south of the West County wine region but is worth mentioning for its great markets and friendly street scene.

We recommend the following businesses if you are in the area.

Andy's Produce and Natural Food Market
1691 Highway 116, three miles north of town
707-823-8661

Fiesta Market
550 Highway 116, just north of downtown
707-823-9735

Food for Thought
6910 McKinley Street, downtown across from town plaza
707-829-9801

Sebastopol Farmers Market
On town plaza, Sundays, 10 a.m. to 1 p.m.

◆

Also of note is a lively flea market that happens every Saturday and Sunday two miles south of Sebastopol on Highway 116. The flea market offers a mix of new and used stuff plus a colorful bunch of produce vendors.

■ Russian River Shopping: Forestville, Guerneville and Monte Rio

Speer's Market
7891 Mirabel Road
At the corner of Highway 116 and Mirabel Road (just off River Road), one mile west of Forestville
707-887-2024
One-stop economy; deli, good breads and produce.

Korbel Champagne Cellars
13250 River Road
Near Guerneville
707-824-7000
Korbel has a fine deli in their brew pub, great take-away, cheeses and condiments.

Food for Humans
16385 First Street
Guerneville
707-869-3612
Organic produce, Village Bakery breads, health and body care.

Coffee Bazaar
14045 Armstrong Woods Road
Guerneville
707-869-9706
Tasty take-away sandwiches and salads.

Bartlett's General Store
9890 Main Street
Monte Rio
707-865-2023
A nice grocery—Village Bakery breads, deli and produce.

■ The Coast, Bodega Bay and Occidental Shopping

In the last decade, we've noticed a renaissance of sorts when it comes to food and the table arts. By looking back, today's producers and purveyors return to traditional methods and sources of raw materials. By looking around, traveling and gathering a world of techniques, they reinvent the market place. By looking forward, they provide us an ever expanding concept of what constitutes cuisine.

While our coastal and rural markets may not offer all the exotic menu choices we often take for granted, such as niçoise olives, cornichons, arugula and numerous choices of lettuce, not to worry. What the country grocers may lack in worldly ingredients and presentation, they make up for with welcome, friendly service and a generous amount of local information.

OCCIDENTAL

Gonnella's Country Mart
707-874-3315
Evergood sausages, Skyhill Napa Chevre, Village Bakery breads.

Facendini's Occidental Market
707-874-3312
Deli, pasta salads, sandwiches, roast chickens and ribs.

BODEGA BAY

Diekmann's Bay Store
1275 Highway 1
707-875-3517
Deli salads, sandwiches, deviled eggs and fried chicken.

Crab Pot
1750 Highway 1
707-875-9970
Smoked fish, and crab in season.

The Tides Wharf
Highway 1
707-875-3652
The newly remodeled Tides Wharf has a great seafood deli/fresh fish market, take-away raw bar, peel-and-eat shrimp, smoked fish—the works, plus restaurant and bayside bar.

TOMALES TOWN

Tomales is a classic crossroads with a great general store, historic roadhouse and a couple of picnic-worthy businesses to mention:

Angel's Cafe
26950 Highway 1
707-878-9909
Good cooking to enjoy in or take away.

Tomales Bakery
707-878-2429
Hot-out-of-the-oven, Thursday through Sunday.

POINT REYES STATION

Wonderfully rural Point Reyes Station is a picnic shopper's dream come true. We highly recommend these fine businesses and a picnic in or around the Point Reyes National Seashore.

Tomales Bay Foods and The Cowgirl Creamery
80 Fourth Street
415-663-9335
Organic produce, world-class take-away food, local cheeses.

Bovine Bakery
11315 State Route 1
415-663-9420
Picnic breads, treats and good coffee.

Palace Market
11300 State Route 1
415-663-1016
One-stop shopping, deli and great locally baked pies.

■ Our Rural General Stores

Still with us from the days of the stage coach lines, the rural general store is a focal point in our crossroads communities. Stop in for supplies and a soda pop at these homey establishments. Some of our favorites are in the following towns and un-incorporated areas:

Jimtown	Dry Creek
Graton	Duncans Mills
Stewarts Point	Freestone
Bodega	Tomales
Valley Ford	Marshall
Olema	

4
Picnic Menus

For the traveler, options for picnic menus depend on where you shop. Healdsburg offers the best selection of prepared and picnic-ready foods, so we will start by suggesting menus with Healdsburg shopping in mind.

I present the menus in the form of a recipe. Use the method as a guide for shopping, but do shop around and keep an eye out for seasonal amendments or substitutions.

■ Spring Vegetable Feast

Menu:

mixed greens vinaigrette with first-crop tricolor radishes

prepared asparagus and/or artichokes

thinly sliced Coppa, Parma or Seranno ham

portion of a soft, fresh cheese like Bellwether Crescenza, or a Telemé, with local strawberries

sweet French baguette

Method:

Downtown Bakery for bread.

Farmers Market, Ansteads Market, or **Oakville Grocery** for greens and radishes.

Oakville Grocery for prepared vegetables, meats and cheeses.

■ Slice of Life and a Piece of Pie Picnic

Take this one out to the ballfield.

Menu:

assorted sandwiches with pickles on the side

potato salad or potato chips

piece of pie

fresh lemonade

Method:

We are partial to Recreation Field in Healdsburg, so this menu method is written for Healdsburg Plaza shopping.

Center Street Café and Deli on the Plaza offers almost everything you might need for this all-American menu, including great fresh-squeezed lemonade in the summer.

Healdsburg Coffee Co. Café, 312 Center Street, for a slice of bumbleberry pie.

Note: This menu is also good for Sunday concerts on the Plaza or a day at Memorial Beach. The historic Recreation Field has baseball all summer and Healdsburg High School Greyhound football in the fall. At football games, feel free to support the excellent barbecue and snack concession run by the Healdsburg High School Booster Club.

■ Summer Salad Picnic

Here's a picnic that begins with a visit to the Farmers Market or a stop along the farm trails for peak-of-season tomatoes, cucumbers and sweet peppers. It's a simple feast of sun-excited vegetable flavors that we suggest you complement with a lively young red wine, slightly chilled.

Menu:

> *a good, rustic loaf of bread*
>
> *tzatziki (see recipes, next chapter)*
>
> *Greek Summer Salad (see recipes)*
>
> *rotisserie or herb-roast chicken (optional)*
>
> *melons*

Method:

This menu works well almost anywhere here in Sonoma County during our prolonged season of delicious, home-grown and multi-hued tomatoes. You can one-stop-shop at most any market, or the **Healdsburg Farmers Market**. However you procure your vegetables, we suggest you plan to wind up at Preston Vineyards for fresh, hearth-baked bread, wonderfully appropriate wines and estate-bottled olive oil. Yasoo!

■ Ends of the Earth Picnic #1

For whale-watching from the overlook at Point Reyes Lighthouse.

The migratory journey of the California Gray Whale puts them off our coast, southbound in December on their way to Baja California calving grounds. From mid-March into May they can be seen heading north. When it's not too foggy, the Point Reyes Lighthouse offers the best vantage point. Otherwise, try Bodega Head (see next picnic) or Salt Point.

Menu:

fresh Drakes Bay oysters with your sauce of choice

assorted crackers

pasta or seasonal-choice salad

apples and pears (plus strawberries in season), with Cowgirl Creamery fresh cottage cheese or creme fraîche

Method:

Stop in Point Reyes Station for your shopping:

Tomales Bay Foods and Cowgirl Creamery for your seasonal salads, organic fruit, fresh cheeses and oyster beverage of choice.

Palace Market for hot sauces, crackers and pasta salads.

Johnson Oyster Company for fresh Drakes Bay oysters. Just off Sir Francis Drake Blvd. on your way to the lighthouse. Call ahead to make sure they'll be open and have oysters available, 415-669-1149.

■ Ends of the Earth Picnic #2

For a wildflower hike on Bodega Head.

Find your way out to the end of the road on Bodega Head. If you visit in late spring or early summer, a fantastic carpet of wildflowers spreads out between the harbor and the vast blue Pacific.

Menu:

romaine leaves with mayoli (see recipes) and marinated artichoke hearts

sourdough bread and brie or chevre

peel-and-eat shrimp

something sweet from the Tides Wharf dessert case

Method:

Tides Wharf for boiled jumbo shrimp, cocktail sauce and dessert.

Diekmann's Bay Store for romaine, mayoli ingredients, cheese, bread and a jar of marinated artichoke hearts. Pick up an extra lemon to season your shrimp and artichoke hearts.

■ Day at the Beach Picnic with the Kids

We like Doran Park on the south side of Bodega Harbor for a picnic when there are kids along. The usually calm, sheltered beach on Campbell Cove complete with tables, windbreaks and fire rings is a nice place for the little ones to enjoy the waterside.

Menu:

snacks of chips, crackers and smoked local salmon

fried chicken

sweet corn roasted in the husks (see recipes)

assorted deli salads and deviled eggs

seasonal melon

picnic lemonade (see recipes)

Method:

As you make your way to Bodega Bay, stop at local farm stands or produce markets for fresh corn, lemons and melons.

Tides Wharf or the **Crab Pot** for smoked local salmon.

Diekmann's Store for fried chicken, deviled eggs, deli salads, lemonade and charcoal.

■ Three Cheese Picnic

Here's a menu for a sunset hike that begins with a stop at Tomales Bay Foods and the Cowgirl Creamery in Point Reyes Station.

Menu:

mixed imported olives

three cheeses—maybe a nice, soft, fresh cheese, a young one, and a hard, aged cheese. Ask the helpful person at the cheese counter to make suggestions, based on the wine you have in mind.

bread

mixed greens vinaigrette (see recipes), or choose one of the seasonal salads available

seasonal fruit: apples, pears, figs, grapes, melons, etc.

Method:

This is a one-stop shopping deal for Tomales Bay and Point Reyes area hikes. **Tomales Bay Foods** has it all, plus tips on picnic places. We like the Bolinas Ridge Trail for this little dairy feast. Find the Bolinas Ridge Trail at a pullout one mile east of the town of Olema on Sir Francis Drake Blvd.

■ Harvest Time Picnic

Find your way out into the vineyards for this meal.

Menu:

> *good bread*
>
> *roast chicken*
>
> *sliced multi-color tomatoes and fresh basil leaves dressed simply with good olive oil and black pepper*
>
> *table grapes*

Method:

The grape harvest coincides with the tail end of tomato season, so the farm stands and farmers markets are good places to shop for your tomatoes,

basil and table grapes. You also have the opportunity to one-stop-shop, and we might suggest **Ansteads Market** in Healdsburg because they prepare our favorite herb and garlic roast chicken. They have local and organic produce, Redwood Hill goat cheese and good bread. From Healdsburg, you can head any direction for your vineyard picnic and great red wines!

5
Recipes for Travelers

H ere are a few recipes that can be prepared at
the picnic table, on a blanket, or in your room
at your lodging. Some of our most memorable meals
have been prepared simply out of our picnic kit on
trains, ferry decks and hotel balconies. Watching
the world go by, passing the bread around, meeting
new people, and conserving your travel funds makes
for a great holiday.

■ Sauces and Dips

The following three basic accompaniments to your
picnic menus are easy to prepare and keep for a
few days if you're traveling with a small ice cooler.

Tzatziki
*A refreshing dip for bread or accompaniment to
roast chicken.*

1. Peel, seed and finely dice:
   1 small cucumber
2. Place a paper napkin over the diced cucumber.
With the palm of your hand, press as much juice
out of the cucumber as you can. Get it dry—it may
take two napkins.
3. Peel and mince very fine:
   **1 small clove of garlic (approximately 1
   teaspoon)**
4. Combine in your salad bowl:
   **8-oz. container plain yogurt (save
   container)**
   cucumber

garlic
1 Tbls. olive oil
pinch of salt

5. Return as much of tzatziki as fits to the yogurt container and keep on ice for your next meal. Dip from what's left in the salad bowl with a nice loaf of crunchy bread.

You can omit or use more garlic according to your taste. You may also keep your eyes out for the wild fennel that seems to grow all over the West County or fresh mint. Pinch a few sprigs if it seems appropriate, mince the leaves and add to your tzatziki for a pleasant change. Note on tzatziki: The more flavorful the yogurt, the better the sauce! We like Redwood Hill Farms brand.

Mayoli
(Cheater's Aioli)

Not the real, authentic French deal, but still delicious on sandwiches, or as a dip for fresh vegetables and crisp romaine. Keep on ice in your cooler and enjoy it over a weekend of picnics.

Note: When you purchase your jar of mayonnaise, plan to use some of it plain, in tuna or chicken salad, or on sandwiches, then you have room to build your Mayoli right in the jar.

1. Remove and use ¼ of an 8-oz. jar of Best Foods Real Mayonnaise®.
2. Mince very fine:
   1 small clove of garlic
3. Combine in the mayonnaise jar:
   remaining mayonnaise
   minced garlic
   juice of ½ small lemon
4. Stir in with a fork:
   enough olive oil to fill the jar
   (approximately 2 Tbls.)

We like to dip leaves of crunchy romaine or

spinach while nibbling pocketknife shavings of Bellwether Farms toscano cheese. Use mayoli as you would mayonnaise, on sandwiches or in salads. Add capers, fresh minced tarragon leaves or minced anchovies for a delicious accompaniment to a rotisserie chicken.

Fresh Tomato Condiment
(Salsa Cruda)

1. Combine in your salad bowl:
   > 1 large tomato, diced (approximately 1 cup)
   > ½ small garlic clove, minced fine
   > 10 leaves fresh basil, torn into small
   > pieces
   > 2 Tbls. olive oil
2. Season to taste with salt and freshly ground black pepper.

Tomatoes in season are one of the many pleasures of Sonoma County's farmers markets and roadside stands. Enjoy salsa cruda spooned onto chunks of fresh, country-style bread, or try topping this combination with little spoons of local goat-milk cheese.

When you're almost done with your spooning and topping, leave a smidge of salsa in your bowl. Build a tasty salad by adding fresh greens, a splash of vinegar, and some olive oil.

Please do add capers and/or anchovies to your salsa cruda, or try some chopped imported olives or spring onion. Add fresh lime, cilantro and minced fresh jalapeño chili. Bring along a bag of corn chips—go wild! Save half a recipe of salsa cruda. Add some bits of leftover bread and a can of cooked white cannellini beans for a rustic treat.

■ Salads

The trick for a picnic chef is finding a way to wash the greens and vegetables. Of course, most markets now have washed mixed greens, salad mixes, sauté mixes, spinach leaves and romaine hearts, the basis of many wonderful salads and a convenient choice for the traveler. However, if you're washing your own fruits and vegetables, use your salad bowl and find water in your room, at gas stations, or at plaza and roadside drinking fountains. Wash your salad greens whole-head, shake dry and store in the salad bowl with the lid on. When preparing picnics at a winery that allows it, ask the tasting room staff about a place to wash your vegetables or a source of potable water.

Greek Summer Salad

A classic, summertime, country-style feast. Serve with hearth-baked bread and tzatziki.

1. Combine in your salad bowl:
   > 1 or 2 medium-size tomatoes, in bite-size chunks
   > 1 small cucumber, peeled and cut into chunks
   > 1 sweet pepper, seeded and cut into chunks
   > ½ small red onion, sliced
   > ¼ lb. Feta cheese, in chunks
   > 15 kalamatas olives
   > pinch salt
2. Dress with:
   > 3 Tbls. olive oil
   > 1 Tbls. red wine vinegar

Traditionally, this salad calls for a pinch of dried oregano. Skip it if you're traveling light, or beg a bit from a friendly waiter at a restaurant. You may also substitute fresh oregano, basil leaves or wild fennel tops. For a delicious rustic variation, coarsely chop

½ bunch of fresh parsley into the salad and pour just a little splash of whatever red wine you're drinking over the whole works. Dip your bread in the bottom of the bowl!

Provençal Salad

Here's a take on the famous salad of Nice that is convenient for the traveler. The hard-cooked eggs in the classic salad can sometimes be replaced by deviled eggs from a deli counter, or you may skip them, or ask at your breakfast café for a couple of hard-boiled eggs to go.

1. Arrange on your serving plate:
   bed of mixed greens, or torn lettuce leaves
   1 medium tomato, quartered
   1 small cucumber, sliced
   1 sweet pepper, seeded and sliced
   2 hard-boiled or deviled eggs, quartered
   1 small can white tuna, in large flakes
   4 green onions, trimmed
   pinch of salt and freshly ground black
      pepper
2. Garnish with:
   very tender raw green or wax beans, if
      available, and
   12 imported black olives
3. Dress with the artichokes and juice from one 6½-oz. jar of marinated artichokes hearts, and:
   1 Tbls. red wine vinegar

Take liberty with this salad and make it a celebration of the season. In early spring, look for tiny asparagus or very fresh fava beans to shell and hull. Summer brings tiny carrots and squash to our markets and farm stands—shopping for this one is half the fun!

Salad Sandwich or Pan Bagnat

If you have some Provençal salad left over, or just plan to make extra, here is a portable meal for a sunset hike.

1. Cut a baguette or flat round loaf of bread in half and hollow out some of the interior to make room for the salad. (Feed the birds with the crumbs, if that seems appropriate.)
2. Spoon and arrange the salad in the hollow and dress with enough juice and oil to moisten but not soak through the bread.
3. Wrap in a plastic bag and keep cool for your evening adventure. Enjoy with a chilled bottle of local Viognier.

Salad of Seasonal Greens Vinaigrette

Fresh mixed tiny lettuces and greens are available almost all year long in most grocery stores. We like to purchase just what we need for one meal, and then get an extra bunch of arugula to add to and enhance the salad. Dress with this simple vinaigrette:

1. Combine:
> 1 small shallot, minced
> pinch of salt
> 1 tsp. prepared mustard
> 1 Tbls. red wine vinegar, or the juice of ½ lemon
> 3 Tbls. olive oil

2. Let this dressing sit for a few minutes to allow the shallot to mellow, then whisk it with a fork and toss your salad. Pass the Chardonnay!

Waldorf Salad

Here's a little blast from the past. Waldorf Salad always takes me back to Bell Park near where I grew up in Detroit, Michigan. Aunt Ethel has brought a big glazed ham for the family picnic, Cousin Marcia has made a Waldorf Salad all by herself, and I'm in big trouble with Mom for playing around too close to the river.

1. Combine in your salad bowl:
       1 cup celery, chopped
       1 large crisp apple, diced
       ½ cup walnuts
       1 cup table grapes, split
       ¼ cup, or so, Best Foods mayonnaise

So now you have shopped for and enjoyed your Waldorf Salad, perhaps with a chilled Fumé Blanc and a ham sandwich. So, what to do with a half a bunch of celery and partial jar of mayo? You can make some mayoli for tomorrow's adventures, and work the celery into a nice Grand Aioli (*Sonoma Picnic*-style).

Grand Aioli
(*Sonoma Picnic*-style)

Here's a suggestion for your day-after Waldorf Salad picnic. Of course we realize that this lunch represents only an approximation of the true French Aioli (Le Beurre de Provence). It's revered the world over. Some gourmets may be scandalized by the thought of Aioli made in a jar, but for us, when on holiday and travel-ing without our mortar and pestle, it works.

Let us begin this small sacrilege with shopping for our feast, the object being to assemble the freshest variety of seasonal raw vegetables to dip in the mayoli. A local farmer's market is your best bet for Sonoma-fresh choices that might include:

sprigs of Italian parsley

arugula leaves or watercress, for spice

asparagus

baby carrots

broccoli

button mushrooms

cauliflower

crisp romaine leaves

cucumber

fennel bulb

hulled tender spring fava beans

multicolored radishes

small new potatoes (raw in moderation)

spring onions

sweet peppers

tiny squash

tomatoes

Dress your presentation of washed and prepared vegetables with freshly ground black pepper, and maybe some pocketknife shavings of hard cheese, like an aged Sonoma jack or Bellwether pepato. We like to take an accompaniment of cracked crab in season, cold roast chicken, or slices of fully cooked mild sausages. Bon appétit!

■ Sandwich Suggestions

Roughly cut slabs of rustic walnut bread, smeared with nice, soft camembert cheese, and a couple of slices of fat, ripe tomato. Season with black pepper, cornichon on the side. Wash it all down with a good, cool, local rosé.

Mild goat cheese on potato bread, Ducktrap pepper-smoked salmon, a few capers and thin shavings of red onion. Iron Horse Classic Vintage Brut, please!

Split ripe black figs in season, mayoli, mixed lettuce greens, cornichon, and thick-cut honey ham on Downtown Bakery hamburger buns. Head for Alderbrook and a chilled Dry Gewurztraminer.

Sweet, fully cooked bay shrimp, mayoli, chopped hearts of romaine, and a nice squeeze of lemon on a split soft roll. Spring onion on the side and a cool Viognier.

Jimtown Store Famous Olive Salad on baguette with a soft, creamy Brie. Just get wine!

◆

The basic drift of this rambling musing on the sandwich is:

- ✎ **Choose the bread with your nose.**
- ✎ **Choose the filling from memory and with your eyes.**
- ✎ **Follow your heart out into the vineyards.**

■ Extras

Sweet Corn Roasted in the Husks

This all-time summer favorite for picnics at the beach begins with fresh corn. Soak or rinse under water for a few minutes before roasting.

1. Prepare a fire of wood or charcoal and let it burn down to a bed of coals and ash.
2. Tuck the whole ears husks and all down into the coals and turn them every so often. If your fire is right and your corn fresh and tender, the whole process only takes ten or fifteen minutes. You are basically steaming the corn in the husks with a little delicious char at the top.
3. Peel back and discard the husks. Dress the ears as you please. Here are some suggestions:

> **Butter and salt, or lime and salt**
> **Rub with lime halves, hot sauce and salt.**
> **Rub with creme fraîche and dress with shavings of a hard sheep-milk cheese.**
> **Dip in buttermilk and dust with cayenne pepper.**

Picnic Lemonade

To perk up an afternoon at the beach, a picnic at the ballfield, or a concert in the city park, here's a summertime suggestion:

1. Purchase in any grocery store:
> **1 gallon spring water**
> **1 12-oz. can frozen lemonade, thawed**
> **2 lemons**
> **2 limes**

2. Use, or pour out, slightly more than one-half of the spring water. (Drink or use to wash vegetables.)

3. Build your beverage in the jug by adding lemonade concentrate.

4. Squeeze the lemons and limes into a cup and add to the jug.

5. Seal, shake and chill at least one hour.

Mom and Dad might want to combine and serve the following mixture over ice:

> **2 parts picnic lemonade**
> **1 part tequila**
> **½ part triple sec**
> **1 lime wedge**

■ Recipe Tips for Traveling Light

Today's vagabond is a lucky soul, what with fresh, seasonal, local farm produce and all the tasty prepared foods conveniently packaged for travel. He or she will find fully cooked and tasty sausages from Gerhards Napa Valley Sausage Company, local cheeses from a multitude of makers, and dips and spreads from a wealth of California producers. Combine all this with world-class, fresh-baked breads, and the picnic chef has a full range of shopping choices from which to craft a meal.

Travel light and take advantage of local deli counters. Purchase imported or local cheeses, cured meats and salamis daily by the ounce. Choose the smallest quantities available for the freshest meals.

Sharing picnic meals with fellow travelers is always a fun option. Preparing for four meals is almost as easy as preparing for two. If you find yourself faced with leftover ingredients, the loss can be taken in stride considering the savings of your picnic meals over the price of restaurant dining.

No need to carry briquettes or build an elaborate fire. It takes just minutes to gather twigs and build a tiny fire for toasting bread or grilling those tasty sausages. Any meat or poultry items that are purchased fully cooked can benefit from a pass over the coals to warm and smoke them up. Build a twig fire only where it is allowed and safe. Only use a provided fire ring or barbecue.

Season your meals with lemon, lime, orange or tangerine. They don't take up much room and a good squeeze of lemon can make a world of dif-ference to a store-bought bean or pasta salad.

Talk to the tasting

room staff when visiting wineries, mention your planned meal, and ask for a wine suggestion. Wonderful food and wine pairings can result. Expand on your discoveries in the comfort of your own kitchen. It's a way to take the trip back home with you.

6

Great Picnic Places: Wineries and Roadside Stops

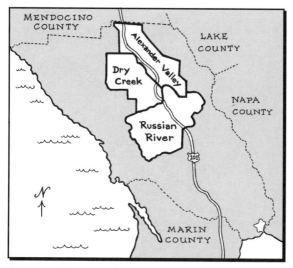

■ Winery Etiquette

We love a wine tour, a day in the countryside, picnicking and a game of bocce. Because this book is basically a picnic guide, we have only listed those wineries that welcome picnickers and that we frequent ourselves. Please don't consider these to be the only places to stop, as the wonderful discoveries you could make in our neighborhood are simply too numerous to mention in this small guide.

When visiting, it's good to keep in mind that the

The heart of **Sonoma Picnic-country**—*Sonoma's western wine appellations. Detailed map follows on page 68.*

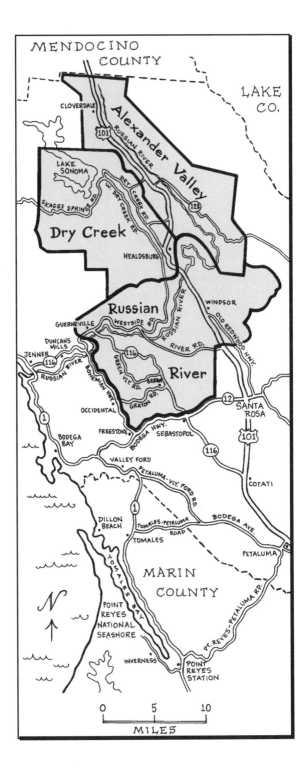

winery is an active business on private property. It is a privilege to be allowed the use of their grounds. Often the winery is also the vintner's home, and they are quite literally sharing their backyards with us, so a few customs are worth mentioning:

- ✎ *Always ask the tasting room staff where to have your picnic.*
- ✎ *It is appropriate to purchase wine when you plan to picnic on the winery grounds.*
- ✎ *Only wines purchased at the winery should be consumed with your meal.*
- ✎ *No grazing in the winery gardens unless you have been specifically invited to do so.*
- ✎ *Please keep in mind the winery hours, and clean up your picnic table before closing time.*
- ✎ *Remember that the winery is like an open-air factory: mind the workers, trucks and forklifts.*
- ✎ *Watch your children.*
- ✎ *Enjoy responsibly and have fun!*

HEALDSBURG AREA

■ Picnic on the Plaza!

Once a thriving Pomo Indian community called Ka'le, or Water Place, the area of the Healdsburg Plaza sits snugly on the bank of Foss Creek in the lower Dry Creek Valley near the big bend in the Russian River. I can imagine this as a perfect picnic place in those pre-European-contact days with a pleasant spring meal of fresh steelhead, split and roasted over an oak-wood fire maybe seasoned with seaweed brought from Bodega Bay, and a side bowl of cattails with wild lily bulbs. In summer, there would be treks to the coast for mussels and surf fish. Back in Ka'le, they would have prepared pit-steamed buckeyes in the fall. The children would gather baskets of grasshoppers trapped and toasted within rings of fire set in the grass, while sweet cakes of berries and wild seeds baked in an earth oven. The fat seasons of spring, summer and fall would be spent drying and preparing foods for the lean season of chill rains and days of no sunshine. Winter would be a time of dance, story, and mystery in the community house, of dried fish and acorn soups, of roasted game birds, of stick games and playing with the babies. I fancy it was somewhat like those snowbound Michigan days I spent having teatime with my grandmother, eating dry biscuits as she spun tales of her youth in old Belfast, of lively music and dances in the days before radio.

By the 1840s, things had changed dramatically for the Pomo of Ka'le. Things had changed a couple of times, but this time it was for keeps–the people's way of life at Ka'le was completely disrupted by surveyors chain and compass, fraternal lodges, and neat picket fences. The survivors' lives were submerged, tumbled and scattered by these waves of change.

Coming not from the vastness of Asia (patiently on foot as the Pomo ancestors did), the new people of the Water Place rushed in by ship and on horseback. Not content to wait for much of anything, these folks had preconceived ideas about the way things should be and wasted no time making Ka'le fit this image. The new people brought with them the ways of their old homes in Mexico and Europe: new animals, new plants, and civil engineering. In 1871, the railroad came to this place, by then known as Healdsburg, with its Spanish-style plaza and redwood sidewalks.

Today, the Plaza is still a wonderful picnic spot, sheltered in the summer beneath the mighty palms and redwood trees so thoughtfully planted for us back in those days of transition. Healdsburg enjoys one of the best examples of early California town planning. The Plaza is the heart of our community, and some of the best food in the world is available just a step across any street to the north, south, east or west. There are no picnic tables but plenty of benches and a verdant lawn.

Note: The City of Healdsburg prohibits the consumption of alcoholic beverages in Plaza Park.

Memorial Beach Park
.75 mile south of the Plaza on Healdsburg Avenue

Long a Russian River tradition, the County erects a summer dam just below the railroad bridge to create a community swimming hole. There are showers, restrooms, shaded tables, barbecue grills and a volleyball court. Note: No alcohol, please.

Giorgi Park and Historic Recreation Field Ball Park
University Street at Piper Street, six blocks northeast of the Plaza

Pick up some sandwiches on the Plaza, then head over to the ball field. All summer the place is hopping day and night with great hometown baseball. In late summer, the place "goes to the dogs," when football coach Tom Kirkpatrick sets the Healdsburg High School Greyhounds to chewing up the competition on Friday evenings. Follow the roar of the crowd to a slice of life! Note: No alcohol in city parks, please.

For information on hometown baseball, call the Boys and Girls Club at 707-433-4479.

When the Healdsburg Greyhounds football team plays home games, you can support the Healdsburg High School Boosters by buying their barbecue and snacks.

Seghesio Family Vineyards
14730 Grove Street
707-433-3579

Picnic under the oaks, maples and firs right in town. Established in 1895, the Seghesio family invites you to enjoy their tasting room and picnic grounds. You might plan your meal with Zinfandel in mind and take a nice stroll out Grove Street.

■ Alexander Valley

The Alexander Valley appellation begins up north of Cloverdale at the Mendocino County line. This world-renowned, long established wine region then follows the Russian River down to the big bend around Fitch Mountain and the town of Healdsburg. You can explore along Highway 101 or get on scenic Highway 128 at Geyserville for a relaxing trip to the southeastern portion of the valley.

Simi Winery

16275 Healdsburg Avenue, about 1.5 miles
 north of the Plaza
707-433-6981

Historic Simi Winery is a pleasant walk or bicycle destination for us Healdsburgers, and we enjoy the cool shade of the redwood trees that tower cathedral-like over the picnic grounds. The tasting room is open daily with tours offered at 11 a.m., 1 p.m. and 3 p.m.

Field Stone Winery and Vineyard

10075 Highway 128, 11 miles east of Healds-burg, in southern Alexander Valley
707-433-7266

Step into the cool dark earth and savor the rich smell of the barrels. Snug underground beneath an oak-covered hill, Fieldstone is a favorite scenic stop. Pack a picnic with Cabernet in mind, sit in the shade of the oaks and enjoy the view.

■ Dry Creek Valley and Lake Sonoma

Dry Creek Valley runs approximately north and south. Two roads run the length of the valley, one east and one west of Dry Creek. Two blocks south of the Healdsburg Plaza turn west on Mill Street, go under Highway 101, and you will see the sign for our first stop in lower Dry Creek.

Alderbrook Vineyards and Winery
2306 Magnolia Drive
707-433-5987

Another favorite walk or bike ride. We enjoy Alderbrook year round, but it's a particularly nice winter or rainy-day picnic place since they have an enclosed and heated verandah with a lovely view to go with their first-class wines.

Mill Creek Vineyards
1401 Westside Road
707-431-2121

Hop over Dry Creek and it's only a skip and a jump down Westside Road to the scenic and shaded picnic deck at Mill Creek, another easy walk or bicycle destination from Healdsburg.

Armida Winery
2201 Westside Road
707-433-2222

The geodesic domes of Armida sit pleasantly up in the hills off the valley floor, and the spacious deck is our picnic place of choice to catch a refreshing breeze on a summer afternoon. We like their Pinot Noir cool from the cellar with mixed olives, goat cheese and crusty bread. Play a spirited bocce game, romp on the

Wino—the leader of the pack at Armida Winery.

lawn with Diva and Wino, the friendly but somewhat larcenous winery dogs (never turn your back on a rotisserie chicken around these two), and enjoy the fantastic view.

◆

From Mill Street in Healdsburg, you cross under Highway 101 to reach Westside Road in the lower Dry Creek Valley. Head north up the valley on West Dry Creek Road for our next picnic places:

Everett Ridge Vineyards & Winery
435 West Dry Creek Road
707-433-1637
www.everettridge.com

For a grand view out over Dry Creek Valley, we get on our bicycles for an easy peddle to this particularly pleasant picnic place. We like the cozy setting surrounded by rolling vineyards, the tasty wines and the company of an amusing gang of acorn woodpeckers who live in the shady heights of a fine old oak. We refer to these woodpeckers as the "demolition crew" since they are busy drilling the historic old barn to pieces. They excavate a finger-size hole, then in autumn fill it with a single acorn as their emergency winter supply. If you look closely, you can see that these birds have been using the old stage stop as their personal granary for many generations.

Lambert Bridge Winery
4085 West Dry Creek Road
707-431-9600

Delicious wines, a friendly crew, and a grand stone fireplace make for a great rain or shine stop in Dry Creek Valley.

Quivira Vineyards
4900 West Dry Creek Road
707-431-8333

Great wines, and a regular stop in Dry Creek Valley for us. We especially like Quivira for late winter

Whitey recumbant, Preston Vineyards

*picnics when the sun is riding low and the barn-wood
wall of the winery catches all the warmth El Sol has
to offer in his stingy season. Plan a picnic with
Zinfandel in mind, and cozy up to that sunny wall.
Summer picnics are worthwhile too in the shade of the
wisteria arbor and the olive trees.*

Preston Vineyards
9282 West Dry Creek Road
707-433-3372

Our all-time favorite picnic place! The idea for
Sonoma Picnic *took shape here during many fine
afternoons in the company of T-Bud, the wise and
ancient winery cat. Red wine, Forno breads, cutthroat
bocce games with out-of-town guests, and more red
wine. Plan a visit and see for yourself. Call ahead for
an update on Lou's freshly baked bread and plan a
meal around a loaf, fresh out of the wood-fired oven.
Bread Hotline: 707-433-4720.*

Pedroncelli Winery
1220 Canyon Road
707-857-3531

*Situated in the hills between Dry Creek and the
Alexander Valley, Pedroncelli is a favorite for all the
usual reasons: tasty wines, beautiful vista from the
picnic grounds, and a bocce court in the heart of Zin
country.*

Dry Creek Vineyards

3770 Lambert Bridge Road

707-433-1000

Lambert Bridge Road crosses Dry Creek mid-valley and runs between West Dry Creek Road and Dry Creek Road.

Opened in 1972, Dry Creek Vineyard exemplifies the true family winery and Sonoma County style. Enjoy exceptionally well made wines, a cordial staff and picturesque picnic grounds.

Lake Sonoma Recreation Area

Take Dry Creek Road north out of Healdsburg, and you will be traveling up the east side of the valley to the base of the impressive Warm Springs Dam. Stop in the Visitor Center or visit the fish hatchery. You'll find plenty of picnic tables, a ballfield, volleyball courts and barbecue grills in the area at the base of the dam. If the looming dam makes you nervous, you'll find another pleasant picnic area near the gravel parking lot south of the Visitor Center at the start of the invigorating 1½-mile Woodland Ridge Loop Trail.

For spectacular vistas and sunset picnics, we recommend you continue on up and around the dam. You will come to a sign for the Stewart's Point-Skaggs Springs Road. Continue straight on Rockpile Road. Three and one-half miles from the Visitor Center, you'll first see a sign for Grey Pine Flat. This is a great place to pull out overlooking the lake, but has no picnic tables. A little farther on up the road, take the pull out for Lone Rock. Here you'll find some tables on a knoll shaded by fine old oaks. A short stroll takes you to another knoll overlooking the lake. It can be absolutely breathtaking at sunset.

The Rules to the Game of Bocce

TOURNAMENT RULES
(Preston House Interpretation)
Courtesy of our friends at Preston Vineyards

1. Select two teams. Teams may be any number of players. Decide among yourselves some system of rotation so everyone gets to play. Half the players from each team roll from opposite ends of the court, alternating rounds.

2. Each team has four balls with matching colors. The small ball is the pallino, or target. Each team takes turns rolling as described in Rule 4.

3. The object of the game is to score the most points, with 12 being game at Preston Vineyards. Points are scored by finishing each round with your team's ball(s) closest to the pallino. One point is scored for each ball closer to the pallino than the closest ball of your opponents. Only the prevailing team scores points each round.

4. Play begins by the flip of a coin. The loser of the toss goes first by throwing out the pallino and then rolling one ball to get it as close to the pallino as possible. The opposing team then rolls as many balls as necessary until one is closer to the pallino than the first team's. Play continues in this fashion with each team besting the other before the turn passes. The round is finished when all balls have been rolled.

5. After each round, the team that scored in the previous round goes first by throwing out the pallino and then rolling.

6. The throw is made from inside the court but behind the first marker. The pallino must be thrown out half way, but should not hit the far end. Throw again if

necessary. If the ball that is thrown hits the far end, it is out of play and is removed from the court for that round. It's OK to hit and move the pallino with your ball or to hit your opponent's ball.

7. Cussing is OK but it should be in Italian. Try not to scuff up the court or bring debris in on your shoes. Red wine is the preferred beverage to accompany the game.

∼∼∼

■ The Russian River and Green Valley

Our Russian River picnic road begins in Healdsburg. Follow Mill Street under Highway 101 and over Dry Creek to Westside Road. Keep left, go past Armida Winery, and you'll pass into the Russian River appellation.

Belvedere Winery
4035 Westside Road
707-433-8236

With terrific Chardonnay and delicious fruit-forward red wines, we like Belvedere's cool redwood grove for picnics on a hot summer day.

Hop Kiln Winery
6050 Westside Road
707-433-6491

In the historic Sweetwater Springs area, the Hop Kiln is a landmark of old stone and timber set by a pleasant little irrigation pond. Enjoy your picnic with a comical gang of colorful hummingbirds and a bottle of Marty's Big Red.

Davis Bynum Winery
8075 Westside Road
707-433-5852

Davis Bynum is a lovely stop for delicious, well-crafted wines and a tranquil, shaded picnic area. To prolong your idyll here, they also have a cottage on the ranch available for rent. Call 800-499-1943, Ext. 10, for reservations.

Iron Horse Vineyards
9786 Ross Station Road
In Green Valley
707-887-1507

From the town of Forestville, go one mile east on Highway 116 to Ross Station Road. Turn right and follow it one more mile down and across the valley to the winery.

Welcome to Iron Horse! Start with a sample of their excellent Classic Vintage Brut. Look out over the valley, and you can taste the harmony of epoch and locality, of season and soil. Try a sip of Chardonnay and savor the best of the winemaker's craft, the years of nurture by many hands, and the blessing of each vintage, unique in the glass.

The Sterling family makes wines for the daily table of life. Each day you wake up to a fresh place setting, sometimes a simple picnic, sometimes a grand banquet. Visit this beautiful ranch and choose a bottle that suits your menu for the day.

Note: If you are planning to picnic at Iron Horse, it's best to call ahead to make sure the picnic area is not in use for a winery function. In the month of September, the picnic area is not available to the public.

Alex of Iron Horse Vineyards—Queen of Green Valley.

Kozlowski Farms
5566 Highway 116
Forestville
707-887-1587
They specialize in homemade jams, jellies and fresh berry and apple pies. Kozlowski Farms also has some picnic supplies, cheese and paté with a pleasant picnic area overlooking Green Valley.

THREE ROADS TO THE COAST

■ Destination Tomales Bay

Start this road to the coast by finding your way to the town of **Occidental**. You might want to plan a breakfast or lunch with a little stroll about. Occidental is a wonderfully Bohemian hideaway. It's an old logging town that has adjusted comfortably to a post-logging and tie-dyed reality.

Head south out of town on the aptly named Bohemian Highway to the town of **Freestone** where you might check out **Java the Hut** for a cup of joe, **Wild Flour Bakery** for great bread or **Osmosis Enzyme Bath** for a mellow place to relax in their tea garden and have a massage. Also, just around the corner on Bodega Highway is **Pastorale** for natural fiber clothing.

Turn right and head west on the Bodega Highway. Three miles west of Freestone on the left is a fine place to picnic, the historic **Watson School Roadside Park**. Sometimes if the coast is socked in and chilly, we'll retreat to the Schoolhouse for our picnic in the sunshine as it lies just east of the summer afternoon fog line.

Bodega Town comes next, situated beautifully in the rolling coastal hills with its historic church and school. It's famous as the location where director Alfred Hitchcock shot *The Birds* in 1962. We always stop for a cold one at **The Casino**. Biker chic since 1939, the Casino is always friendly, positively for real, and a treasure alongside a highway that's custom-built for two wheels.

One mile west of Bodega, turn left on State Route 1. The town of **Valley Ford** is four miles down the road. Six miles south of Valley Ford you'll hit the town of **Tomales**, also a cool stop for a cold one at the **William Tell House**, circa 1877. Perhaps a sniff through **Mostly Natives** would be nice; they grow and sell plants appropriate for our climate. At Tomales is the cutoff to Elephant Rocks and Dillon Beach. Turn right here for a visit to the mystical, dare I say downright trippy, rock formations overlooking the mouth of Tomales Bay. Surfers know Dillon Beach for great surf and the occasional donation to the Great White. It's worth a detour and a poke around for sure.

Continuing south on State Route 1, you will pass **Nick's Cove** and **Tony's**, both classically coastal establishments. Next comes **Hog Island Oyster Company** (see pages 37–38) and **Millerton Point**, a fine roadside stop where you can picnic with the osprey and hike along the bayside. In late fall and early winter, the osprey head south of the border, but you might catch a local shore fisherman pulling a leopard shark or a sturgeon out of the bay.

Point Reyes Station is the official end of this road to the coast, but should only be the beginning of your explorations in and around the Point Reyes National Seashore.

A drive to **Tomales Bay** is one of our favorite weekend adventures. As a matter of fact, on this twelfth day of March the winter of 1998, Janette and I have just returned from an evening's campover in the lovely redwoods of **Samuel P. Taylor State Park**. We enjoyed three great picnics along the way. First we had a sunset snack of goat-milk cheeses, olive salad, bread and fruit on the Bolinas

Ridge Trail, then a camp dinner of steamed artichoke with mayoli. We brought along precooked duck breasts and crisped them over a redwood twig fire. We sliced them thin over a bed of mixed greens vinaigrette and had chocolates and Cabernet for dessert in the moonlight. *Note:* when camping and cooking at Samuel P. Taylor State Park, expect guests in the form of very bold raccoons who think nothing of climbing right up on the table while you're dining.

In the morning after tea, we drove out to the light-house at Point Reyes to watch the whales passing on their way back up north. We stopped at Johnson Oyster Company for fresh Drakes Bay oysters on our way to the Point for an ends of the earth picnic of half-shell oysters, soda crackers and ice-cold beer.

It was one of those spectacular, calm, clear and warm winter days. The whales were passing so close to the rocks we could look down to see the whole animals swimming beneath the surface.

■ Destination Bodega Bay via Occidental

Begin this road to the coast in the town of **Occidental.** You'll see Coleman Valley Road head-ing west up the hill behind **Negri's Italian Dinners.** Not recommended for trailers or RVs, this narrow winding road affords some of the most spectacular views in the area. Two miles up the road, keep right on Coleman Valley Road. You'll go about three more miles before you reach the top of the hill and the grand panorama of wind-blown range lands falling away to the beautiful Pacific. You can look to the southwest over a tiny sliver of Tomales Bay all the way out to Point Reyes. This is all private land up here, but the road has lots of places you can pull off and enjoy the view. We like this road in early spring, around the first of April, as the place is alive with bluebirds, wild iris and fresh green grass after the months of winter rains. Please mind the cows in open range country. You cross miles of unfenced pasture up here.

Coleman Valley Road comes down off the hill to intersect Highway 1 six miles north of Bodega Bay. You'll see several splendid places in Sonoma Coast State Beach to pull off and enjoy the beach before you get into town. One mile south on Highway 1 is **North Salmon Creek Beach and Lagoon**, a good spot on a calm day for blanket picnics on the fine sandy beach. If it's a windy day, we go on another mile and a half to **Bodega Dunes Campground**, which has a nice day-use area with tables and barbecue grills somewhat sheltered behind the dunes from a beautiful broad beach.

You can continue on to **Bodega Head**, a fascinating promontory that shelters the fishing harbor at Bodega Bay. Turn right onto Eastside Road on the north end of town. This will take you down to the harbor and Westside Road, which leads out to **Bodega Head Park**. There you have three excellent picnic areas to choose from. The first is at **Hole in the Head**, a deep duck pond excavated for a nuclear power plant that was never built. It overlooks the harbor breakwater and Campbell Cove on the bay side. We like this spot on a windy or gray day. It has tables where you can watch thousands of sea birds making their living in and around the harbor. From Hole in the Head, the park road climbs to the top of Bodega Head where the first parking lot on the left marks the start of a dramatic bayside trail where you might find a secret picnic table tucked into the brush overlooking the harbor and bay. You can also continue on to the end of the park road for calm-day blanket picnics on the open bluffs overlooking the pounding sea. Take the trails north or south for whale-watching and hawk-spotting amid a wealth of wind-stunted wildflowers.

South of Bodega Bay, follow the signs to **Doran Regional Park** for another Bodega Bay picnic option at the very end of this road to the coast (see page 51.)

■ Destination Bodega Bay via Guerneville and Jenner

At the town of **Guerneville** where this road to the coast begins, River Road meets Highway 116 which continues down the Russian River to the sea. We like to stop in Guerneville for a stroll around this colorful river resort community. During the summer months, the population swells with holiday-makers and families enjoying the thousands of little vacation cabins hidden away in the canyons surrounding the town. Lots of family memories lurk in them thar hills. I can imagine generations of first kisses down around a campfire on the river, while Moms and Dads were up to more adult high jinks in those cabins and in the bars and taverns of Guerneville and Monte Rio.

From downtown Guerneville, you can head north on the Armstrong Woods Road for a side trip to **Armstrong Redwoods State Reserve** and **Austin Creek State Recreation Area**, where you'll find plenty of great picnic places as well as hiking, beautiful old trees, clear streams and camping of both the drive-in and back-country kinds.

Back in Guerneville, head west on Highway 116 toward Monte Rio. If you want to explore the coastal hill country north of the Russian River, you can take a scenic side trip up either Old Cazadero Road or Austin Creek Road, winding north to connect with either the King Ridge Road or the Fort Ross Road and a very winding but scenic route to Fort Ross or Salt Point on the coast. We suggest you have plenty of gas and a good map for this trip.

Four miles west of Guerneville, Highway 116 enters the resort community of **Monte Rio**. Main Street heads south, turning into the Bohemian Highway which runs through the redwoods to the towns of Occidental and Freestone. Continue west from Monte Rio on Highway 116 for six miles to the intriguing hamlet of **Duncans Mills**, population

85, with its several little shops, the great **Duncans Mills General Store** and the **Blue Heron Restaurant & Tavern**.

Heading west another few miles on Highway 116, the countryside opens up to broad, rolling, coastal range until the Russian River meets the sea at the town of **Jenner**. Here Highway 116 ends at Coast Highway 1, giving you the option of heading north or south along the spectacular coast.

Heading south on Highway 1 through Sonoma Coast State Beach, the first good beach stop is **Goat Rock Beach**. From here you can hike out on the spit of sand to the mouth of the Russian River. Mind the harbor seals and watch for rogue waves! The cardinal rule on the north Pacific Coast is "Never turn your back on the ocean!" Rogue, oversize waves can strike at any time, sweeping unsuspecting beachcombers out to sea. Harbor seals, which hang out in a herd at the mouth of the Russian River, are wild animals and should never be approached. That especially goes for their babies, whose moms leave them alone on the beach while they go catch a fish dinner for the family.

Heading down the Coast Highway from Goat Rock, you'll come to **Wright's Beach** in about four miles. It has a day-use/picnic area and a popular campground. Continue south to **Duncans Landing,** where if you turn out, you'll see a rock outcrop which has a couple of caves filled with the debris of centuries of Native American home-making. Just five miles south of the Russian River, this special rock offered a fine place to camp while gathering the bounty of the sea. Today picnic tables and toilets provide modern conveniences for visitors to this ancient picnic ground. Just south of Duncans Landing, a lone picnic table perches atop **Rock Point**.

One-half mile further south sits another lone table at **Gleason Beach**. We like to call this picnic spot "contractor's folly overlook," or "the beach where all the money goes." Look south to see Mother Nature at work tidying up after a number of harried homeowners who, for whatever reason, continue to defy her with rock, wood, concrete and an acre of multicolor plastic tarps. We find this a bittersweet picnic place best reserved for days when you might want to brood on the tenuous hold we have here on the fair blue sphere, our times a brief struggle with the waves and the imponderable winds of change . . . hey! What the heck, let's continue on the road, south past **Portuguese Beach, Carmet Beach, Arched Rock Beach, Coleman Beach, Miwok Beach** and **North Salmon Creek Beach**, to a cold beer overlooking Bodega Harbor at **The Tides Wharf Bar** . . . ahh, now that's living!

THE NORTH SONOMA COAST

■ Highway 1 North from Jenner to Fort Ross State Historic Park and Gualala

I'd like to describe one of our special winter days! It's Tuesday, the twelfth of December 1998, the sun's just coming up, the tea kettle's on, it's a crisp, clear morning, and I've packed an overnight bag to head for a tiny cabin overlooking the sea. Janette has volunteered to work on our regular days off, so I'm left to my own devices.

We have a friend who lives just north of Gualala in Mendocino County. He built his shack there out of cast-offs and barnyard salvage. The place is quite rustic with kerosene lamps and an antique iron shepherd's stove. Our friend generously lets me use this cozy retreat which comes complete with two comical little dogs and a black cat named Raven. I plan on finishing this last road story there, which completes my work on *Sonoma Picnic*. I'm going to cook a pot of Hobo's Stew, bake buttermilk biscuits, and begin work on my next project, *Mendocino Picnic*, by kerosene lamplight with a bottle of Wild Hog Zinfandel.

To begin this road to the Mendocino County line, find your way down the Russian River to the town of Jenner. I've had a great drive today, past the vineyards and through the redwoods. As far as picnic shopping is concerned, I might suggest you shop on your way to Jenner for your lunch, or you can put something together at the world class **Stewarts Point General Store**, or drive on through to the Gualala/Anchor Bay area where there's some great picnic fare available as well.

For my shopping, I've made a short side trip to **The Tides Wharf**, just south of Jenner at Bodega Bay. It's the heart of our crab season and a splendid day for eating cracked Dungeness crab cooked fresh daily on the docks, with cocktail sauce, a box of crackers, and an ice-cold beer. It also is whale watching season, so with my crab and beer in the cooler I'm going to drive north along the sparkling sea until I find a lookout and some whales to watch.

Just north of Jenner, past the **River's End Inn and Tavern**, there's a pullout overlooking the long beach and dunes at the mouth of the Russian River. Today nearly one hundred assorted pinnipeds are sunning on the river bank with vast flocks of seagulls milling about, and a dozen brown pelicans doing their gangling, break-neck fishing dives into the calm backwaters behind the sand dunes. This is a great spot to enjoy a birds-eye view of all the critters who make their living in and around this dramatic juncture of fresh and salt water. It's not much of a picnic place, so I'm heading north about twelve miles to **Fort Ross State Historic Park**.

About half way to the fort, the twisting highway climbs to its 600-foot summit where the **Vista Trail** on the left offers bird's eye views and picnic tables along a ¾-mile paved path that's wheelchair accessible. The coast road descends from there to Fort Ross.

One day in March of 1812, a surprising sight greeted the Kashaya Pomo who made their homes on the bluffs above what's now known as Fort Ross Cove. A large sailing ship came to anchor and disgorged more than a hundred people who, from that day forward, would change life considerably for the Pomo. The arrival of these colonists from far off Russia introduced a whole new way of doing things, and the beginning of a Russian presence that would last until 1841. The local Pomo people lived agreeably with the Russian settlement and were paid for their labor and the use of the land. The descendants of these Kashaya Pomo continue to live and work along this remote and rugged coast.

Today the site of Fortress Ross is a beautiful 3386-acre State Park with 20 primitive campsites (first come, first served, open April through November), some fine picnic places, and the modern Interpretive Center beside the restored fort. While there's not much in the way of a developed trail system, you're free to wander anywhere within park boundaries. I suggest you pick up a map in the Interpretive Center and explore; one trail leads to picnic areas by the old ranch house, then drops down to the beach in Fort Ross Cove and more picnic tables. You may want to stroll about the old Russian orchard or through a lovely grove of redwoods smack on the San Andreas fault. The pullout for the latter two lies not quite a mile east of Highway 1 on Fort Ross Road which bisects the park. From there you get a dramatic view back down to the fort and the coast.

If you don't have one already, the Interpretive Center at Fort Ross is a good place to pick up a copy of *The Hiker's hip pocket Guide to Sonoma County* by Bob Lorentzen. Bob describes in detail the natural history, flora, and fauna on four hikes within the park and along the fascinating San Andreas fault rift zone.

This morning the groundskeeper has a nice fire going in the barbecue pit inside the fort. The smell of the smoke on this sunny winter day sets a grand mood for wandering around these old buildings. I'm tempted to break into my picnic here, but I haven't spotted any whales yet so I'll leave this nineteenth century reverie for another day's lunch and head north.

Four miles north of Fort Ross is **Stillwater Cove Regional Park**, which has campgrounds with showers, trails, pleasant picnic spots and a good path down to the beach of the splendid little cove.

Next comes **Salt Point State Park** with camping and plenty of picnic possibilities on 6,000 acres of mixed terrain along six miles of gorgeous coast. Salt Point is truly a park for all seasons with fantastic clear, dry winter days like today, amazing spring and summer wildflowers, plus some of the best mushroom hunting in fall and winter. We like to pop into the **Salt Point Bar and Grill** for a sunset drink after a day cruising around the woods and exploring the numerous little hideaway beaches in the park.

One mile north of the Salt Point State Park campground, look for the sign to **Fisk Mill Cove**. You have two choices here—keep to the left and you'll find a dozen shaded picnic tables and barbecue grills within earshot of the pounding sea. A fine trail threads down through the woods to the beach, but the real treasure here is a blanket picnic spot we call Lazy Boy Rock which overlooks the cove. Follow the steps and path until you see a wood fence along the sea bluff. Look around for a fine old sandstone boulder with the bleached skeleton of a mighty pine laying behind it. You'll find soft grass and the smooth rock for your back. This is a great spot to cozy with your sweetheart at sunset. You might want to bring two blankets and stay awhile.

If you keep to your right when you pull off Highway 1 on the Fisk Mill Cove access road, you'll find more pleasant shaded tables with barbecue grills and the bluff trail back to the cove, ⅜ mile.

My next stop is the **Stewarts Point General Store**, an intriguing break from the road. It sits at the junction of Highway 1 and the scenic and twisting Stewarts Point-Skaggs Springs Road that heads east to Lake Sonoma and Dry Creek Valley. The General Store dates back to 1868 and has been in the same family since 1881. It's the granddaddy of general stores. You can get anything from your basic produce, cheese and sausage to guns and ammo, hunting or fishing license, abalone endorsement, hooks, lines and a really complete selection of sinkers. Oh, let me go on . . . you might find things the owners didn't even know they had. Need a mailbox? How 'bout a gas tank for your boat? Rat trap, tea kettle, a great choice of picnic enamelware, rubber boots, spark plugs, baby diapers . . . stop in and see for yourself! I picked up a jar of spicy pickled beans and a bottle of Wild Hog Zinfandel for my supper that night.

Wild Hog Vineyard is a mom and pop operation hidden away in the hills east of Fort Ross. They are not open to the public, but if you spot their distinctive label in the shops, treat yourself to a little something from the rugged coastal highlands.

Just beyond Stewarts Point you'll be passing through **Sea Ranch**. Sea Ranch is all private property with a number of neatly maintained public access areas with paths that lead down to the various beaches. These access areas are part of the **Sonoma County Regional Parks** system, and a single $3.00 day-use fee gets you into all of them. One of our favorites is **Stengel Beach**. A short walk takes you to the bluff where a waterfall dances out over a mudstone ledge to crash directly into the rock-strewn surf when the tide is high.

About a mile and a half north of Stengel Beach, just past the Sea Ranch North Fire Station, take the time to check out the **Sea Ranch Chapel**! Enjoy some quiet reflection in your own personal sanctuary of sculptured wood and beach stone.

Today, the sun is pouring in, euphorically, through the stained glass and, out of the total silence, in the midst of daydreaming, a little inner voice, like a church mouse on helium, whispers, "Lunch . . . Jack, it's time to eat!"

The whales oh, yes! There is one more stop before we run out of Sonoma County and cross the Gualala River into Mendocino County. Three miles north of the Chapel, look for the sign to the Visitor Center at **Gualala Point Regional Park**. From the Visitor Center, take the paved path to the beach. Follow the park boundary fence line down through the pines and off the paved path until you get to the bluffs overlooking the sea. From here you can turn south and hike out to **Whale Watch Point**, but I prefer to follow the bluff path north to a picnic on **Beauty & Hildegarde's Bench**. This bench, dedicated by someone with love to their dogs, overlooks a roaring cove. Far out to sea I spy the telltale spout of a southbound gray whale. I salute whales and my good fortune to be enjoying this vista with an ice-cold bottle of Red Tail Ale. I have the company of two pretty, plumb-eyed white-tail does who are munching away on lush winter grass about 30 feet behind me. A pair of ravens tumble on the wind.

With some difficulty I get myself up off this five-star dog bench to make my way to the grocery store in Gualala and on to the cabin so I can get a fire lit and my supper started.

I hope you've found some helpful tips in this little narrative. If you have, I invite you to look for a copy of *Mendocino Picnic* wherein I'll continue the story of this fine day with a recipe for the Hobo's Stew that's now bubbling away on the wood stove. Cheers!

Annapolis Winery
26055 Soda Springs Road
Annapolis
707-886-5460
Completely off the beaten track on a hilltop

overlooking a gorgeous coastal mountain valley, and well worth the long but scenic drive, we highly recommend a picnic visit to this homey family winery. Gas up your rig, load in a picnic, and head into the hills for delicious wine pairings way out in the middle of the woods.

From Highway 1 about nine miles south of Gualala, take the Annapolis Road seven miles to Soda Springs Road, then follow signs to the winery. Each and every vintage is unique from these lovely sixteen acres of vines.

The Horses and Hogs Run

Let me introduce my adventure companion, Mr. Fred Carlo. Fred is a fellow of many qualities, wise like an Italian grandfather, and funny like a Jewish uncle. He hails from New York State and apparently cannot help himself. It seems at birth he was handed a life sentence: go out into the world, have fun, make people happy. In keeping with the terms of his sentence, Fred is a cook (one of the best I know) and a wizard with the pig. There isn't a better Italian salumière than this guy, and hardly anything makes more people happy than Fred's hellishly spiced fresh Italian sausages, home-cured prosciutto and salami. Plus, he looks great in an apron, beaming over a perfectly roasted porchetta.

One late winter day, Fred showed up pretty much unannounced. When you live in paradise, house guests happen.

I had a couple of days off from work, so I decided to take Fred to the coast along a favorite route, the Horses and Hogs run from Iron Horse Vineyards in Green Valley, for a bottle of their excellent Classic Vintage Brut, to Hog Island Oyster Company on Tomales Bay, for an eat-them-at-the-source oyster feast.

From Healdsburg, off we went down Eastside Road to Iron Horse Ranch. Our pal winemaker David Munksgard treated us to a barrel tour extraordinaire. We tasted the new wines, a legacy of soil and wood, of season and craft. Fred remarked, "Now this is the way to start the day!"

Leaving Iron Horse with a chilled bottle of bubbly, we took the Graton Road down through the redwoods to the town of Occidental on the old Bohemian Highway. The Bohemian Highway took us through Freestone to the Bodega Highway. Here the countryside began to change with open, rolling rangelands and stunted, windswept trees tucked down into the draws. You get the sense of getting close to the coast. Wobbly new lambs bounced around in the pastures, hawks perched on the fence posts, kites and kestrels hunted the fields for tiny four-legged picnic fare.

"Hang a louie on the Valley Ford/Freestone Road," I suggested. I was savoring my role as navigator in the cramped cockpit of Fred's hot little red 'pasta e fagioli' of an Italian sports car. The car and driver became one with the sweep and turn of this scenic country road. From the look on his face, I suspected Fred was back in Italy somewhere out of San Remo, tooling down the Ligurian back roads of his dreams, eating tiny black olives and spitting the pits out the window.

We turned onto Coast Highway 1, and at the town of Tomales made a right turn on Dillon Beach Road. We spent an hour poking around the wonderfully mysterious Elephant Rocks, a perfect place to take a break from the road, overlooking the wild bar at the mouth of Tomales Bay. We reflected on the luck of our lives that we should be here now to ponder these profound old stones.

Back on Highway 1, we headed south to the town of Marshall (population 50), midway down Tomales Bay and home to the Hog Island Oyster Company. We enjoyed sunshine on the bayshore, a bottle of habañero salsa, a box of soda crackers, deliciously crisp sparkling wine, and a world of oyster choices: Sweetwater, Atlantic, Kumamoto and European. We shucked a whole bunch, fresh and tangy, right out of the holding tank.

Whether you bring Hog Island oysters to Iron Horse Ranch or the Iron Horse Brut down to the bay, I've found nothing quite like this "Horses and Hogs" combination for stimulating conversation. Fred and I, a couple of former line-cooks, yukked it up about the good old days. For us, those were the late seventies and eighties in the restaurants of Portland, Oregon. Yak, yak ". . . and what about the night Patrick dropped the bottle of brandy into the deep fryer." Hoot, hoot, blah, blah. Though we could have made much more money in the company of regular guys at the mill, or in the mud of a construction site, we both found our calling in the relative comfort and rush of the kitchen and the eccentric mix of wait-staff, bartenders, bakers and stoned-out busboys.

As Helios raced west on his low winter track, Fred and I headed east on the Tomales-Petaluma Road to hook up with Highway 101 for the express route home and a quick stop in the back bar of Volpi's in Petaluma. A former speakeasy behind Volpi's Italian Market, the historic back bar is a must stop for shots and beers where the faithful, the latter day Dionysians engage in their daily ritual of gossip and wise cracking. Volpi's back bar is a no-frills kind of shrine, but they do have an impressive collection of musty old stag heads mounted on the walls. And yes, that is a stuffed golden eagle behind the bar. And yes, there are a half-dozen accordions and a piano.

The place really swings when the locals get the spirit!

7
Dining Out

A guide to the neighborhood would be incom-
plete without a mention of our favorite restaurants and grills. We advise calling for reservations,
particularly for dinner.

■ Healdsburg, Geyserville and Cloverdale

Restaurant Charcuterie
335 Healdsburg Avenue
Healdsburg
707-431-7213
Lunch and dinner
Great lively café atmosphere, wine list and menu.

Ravenous
117 North Street
Healdsburg
707-431-1770
Lunch and dinner; call for hours
Wonderful cooking; cozy, cozy fun!

Bistro Ralph
109 Plaza Street
Healdsburg
707-433-1380
Lunch and dinner
Great upscale cooking; best martini on the planet.

Acre Café & Lounge

420 Center Street
Healdsburg
707-431-1302
Creative cooking, a cozy bar with a fireplace for winter nights and lovely backyard for summertime dining.

Felix & Louie's

106 Matheson
Healdsburg
707-433-6966
Lunch, dinner and late-night
Wood-fired pizza oven and a lively bar.

Taqueria El Sombrero

245 Center Street
Healdsburg
707-433-3818
Lunch, dinner and food to go
Not to be missed, down-home delicious and economical.

Bear Republic Brewing Company

345 Healdsburg Avenue
Healdsburg
707-433-2337
Good brews. Lunch, dinner and live music.

Healdsburg Coffee Company Café

312 Center Street
Healdsburg
707-431-7941
Homey breakfast and lunches

Center Street Café & Deli

304 Center Street
Healdsburg
707-433-7224
Breakfast and lunch
The place on the Plaza for breakfast, fresh juice and smoothies.

Catelli's "The Rex"
241 Healdsburg Avenue
Healdsburg
707-433-6000
Lunch and dinner
Great wine list and bar. An institution since 1937, Catelli's has long been the restaurant of choice for many Alexander Valley growers and winemakers. As this book went to press, the venerable Catelli's opened in this new location in Healdsburg. While Geyserville's loss will be Healdsburg's gain, look for more good cooking at the old Catelli's location, 21047 Geyserville Avenue. The word on the street says that several talented local chefs have their sights set on the old place.

Pick's Hamburgers
117 S. Cloverdale Boulevard
Cloverdale
A classic drive-in with counter service at five outdoor stools. Pick's has been locally owned and operated since 1923.

■ Russian River

Farmhouse Inn & Restaurant
7871 River Road
Near Forestville
707-887-3300
Where the vineyards meet the redwoods. A wonderful place for dinners, weddings and events. Call for information.

Topolos at Russian River Vineyards
5700 Gravenstein Hwy North (Highway 116)
Green Valley
707-887-1575
Lunch and dinner
Great patio dining and gold-medal wines.

Applewood Inn & Restaurant
13555 Highway 116
Guerneville
707-869-9093
Dinner, weddings and events
Charming decor and great food.

Willowside Café
3535 Guerneville Road
707-523-4814
Dinner only, Wednesday through Sunday
A favorite stop for dinner. The Willowside's creative cooking is only fifteen minutes east of Iron Horse Vineyards on the road to Santa Rosa. Reservations highly recommended.

■ Occidental and the Coast

The town of Occidental on the way to the coast has an intriguing little group of businesses, all clustered along a two-block stretch of the Bohemian Highway. If you're planning to dine, we suggest you take a stroll and pop into the place that best suits your fancy. The whole town is something of a dining Mecca, hidden away in the redwoods and locally famous for old-fashioned family-style Italian dinners.

Altamont Bar & Grill
Bohemian Café
Howard Station Café
Negri's Italian Dinners
Occidental Hotel
Union Hotel Restaurant

JENNER

River's End
11051 Highway 1
707-865-2484
Breakfast, lunch and dinner
Good cooking and a pleasant bar with a spectacular view overlooking the mouth of the Russian River.

BODEGA BAY

Dog House
537 Highway 1
Around the corner on Smith Brothers Road
707-875-2441
Extra points for fun and friendly! Bayside dogs, burgers, fries and beer. Check out the equally friendly Ruby's Porthole, right next door, for coffee and ice cream.

Lucas Wharf Restaurant and Bar
595 Highway 1
707-875-3522
Lunch and dinner

Sandpiper
1410 Bay Flat Road
707-875-2278
Open daily for breakfast, lunch and dinner

Tides Wharf & Restaurant
835 Highway 1
707-875-3652
Newly remodeled, but with that same old hung-out-over-water coastal style.

Duck Club at Bodega Bay Lodge
103 Highway 1
707-875-3525
Great, tasteful dining overlooking the bay.

TOMALES

Angel's Café
26950 Highway 1
707-878-9909
A sweet little roadside stop. Great picnic take-away too.

TOMALES BAY

Approximately four miles south of the town of Tomales on Highway 1, you will come to a couple of classically coastal establishments set on beautiful Tomales Bay. Both of these wonderful family businesses are open mostly for weekend trade so the hours of operation may vary with the season. We highly recommend both these cozy places famous for oysters and seafood. Call to see when they're open.

Nick's Cove
415-663-1033

Tony's Seafood Restaurant
415-663-1107

POINT REYES STATION

Tomales Bay Foods
80 Fourth Street
415-663-9335
The best take-away foods on the coast!

Pine Cone Diner
60 Fourth Street
415-663-1536
Homey breakfast and lunch.

Taqueria La Quinta
11285 State Route 1
415-663-8868
Fun and economical lunch and dinner.

8

The Sonoma Valley: Exploring the East County

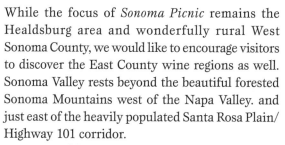

While the focus of *Sonoma Picnic* remains the Healdsburg area and wonderfully rural West Sonoma County, we would like to encourage visitors to discover the East County wine regions as well. Sonoma Valley rests beyond the beautiful forested Sonoma Mountains west of the Napa Valley. and just east of the heavily populated Santa Rosa Plain/ Highway 101 corridor.

Separated from our West County area by the facts of geography and the vagaries of history, Sonoma Valley is easy to reach on day trips to the historic

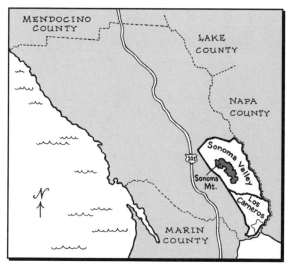

Sonoma's southern wine appellations offer delightful picnic fare in a variety of venues. Detailed map follows on page 102.

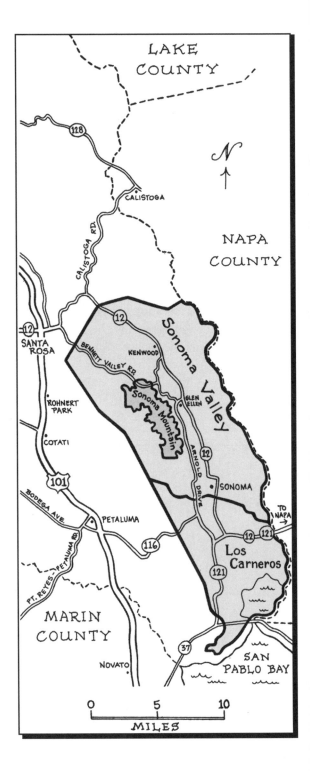

wineries, towns and other points of interest. We suggest you explore now, and plan a longer stay with our friends to the east in the future.

■ Getting There

Just 46 miles north of San Francisco on Highway 101, State Highway 12 heads east into the Sonoma Valley. You can also get there from the south off Highway 101 at Novato—take State Highway 37 east to State Highway 121 and go north to Sonoma. Or from Petaluma, take State Highway 116 east.

From the Healdsburg area, reach the Sonoma Valley by heading down U.S. Highway 101 to Santa Rosa and traveling east on Highway 12, the Sonoma Highway, to the Kenwood area at the very top of the Sonoma Valley.

■ Where To Stay

Accommodations in the Sonoma Valley run the full range from elegant luxury hotels and spas to cozy, affordable B&Bs. We suggest you call, write or visit the very helpful staff at the Sonoma Valley Visitors Bureau. They'll be happy to send you the handy Sonoma Valley Visitors Guide which includes a little historical background and a good list of up-to-date lodging, event, winery, camping and restaurant information.

> **Sonoma Valley Visitors Bureau**
> 453 First Street East
> Sonoma, CA 95476
> 707-996-1090
> Open 7 days a week on the Plaza.

◆

ALMOST PARIS

One fine day after harvest, Janette informs me there is a girls' weekend coming up, and maybe there is something that I need to do that doesn't involve actually being in the house for a night or two.

I look forward to cooking a big dinner on their first night. I get to entertain, read a new story, sing a couple of new songs. The girlfriends are generally amused. I make sure to have plenty of Iron Horse sparkling wine on ice to keep the amusement factor up. Having depleted my repertoire of entertaining material after one night, I'm happy to slip out for some guy time and leave the house and Healdsburg to the ladies.

A couple of nights in Reno usually springs to mind when I'm presented with an opportunity like this: The Biggest Little City in the World, all night low-rolling, nickel slots, free drinks, and 99¢ steak and eggs—the perfect retreat when your house is full of girlfriends, all going on about those crazy days of the old Mt. Hood gang.

Since I'm facing a deadline with my publisher, I decide Reno can wait, and instead book a favorite room at the historic old Sonoma Hotel right on the Plaza in Sonoma town. I like Room 22 on the third floor. It has a writing desk and a window on the Plaza. The hotel is very European in style, affordable and friendly.

In the morning a gang of loudmouth roosters bragging over on the Plaza make sure I'm up to catch the dawn. But the hotel has good steam heat and a bath down a hallway that is splashed with rainbows as the sun pours in through a fine-cut glass window. Hemingway in Paris didn't have a better set up. The only thing missing is a chestnut vendor—the gnarly old bird wearing three sweaters, a wool cap and jacket. Where is that guy? . . . Toasting a perfect vision of the 1920s over hot coals on the street corner.

―⁓⁓―

Since we live only an hour drive from the Sonoma Valley, we rarely need to take a room when we visit, but we'd like to provide a short list of favorite places where you might enjoy staying. A night in Sonoma Valley for us is like a little vacation right in our own backyard.

The Sonoma Hotel

110 W. Spain Street
Sonoma
707-996-2996
See "Almost Paris" on previous page.

Swiss Hotel

18 W. Spain Street
Sonoma
707-938-2884
Five lovely rooms, and the coziest bar in the county, plus a first class restaurant. Reserve early!

Sonoma Mission Inn and Spa

18300 State Highway 12
Boyes Hot Springs
707-938-9000
Sonoma Valley deluxe with spa packages, fine dining and a lively café.

■ Camping

Sugarloaf Ridge State Park

2605 Adobe Canyon Road
Kenwood
For reservations call: 1-800-444-7275, or access Park Net online at www.parknet.com. For further park information, call: 707-833-5712 or 707-938-1519.

Located north of State Highway 12 and seven miles east of Santa Rosa above Kenwood, the park's 2,700 acres offer 50 developed campsites and a picnic ground. Twenty-five miles of trails afford clear-day views of the Sierra Nevada and the Golden Gate Bridge.

Weather permitting, the **Sonoma Cattle Company** *offers daily trail rides, sunset rides, and summer full moon rides on selected trails within the park. Call 707-996-8566 for details.*

The **Ferguson Observatory**, *located in the park, offers scheduled free viewing through its marvelous 40-inch telescope. Call the observatory for information: 707-833-6979.*

■ Bicycle Touring

Once you get settled in lodging or camp, consider a bicycle tour, an excellent way to see the Sonoma Valley which has more designated bike paths than elsewhere in Sonoma County. For more information about bicycle travel, contact one of the bike shops or bike tour operators listed in **Chapter 2**. They can help in a variety of ways, from pointing you in the right direction to renting you bikes to taking you on a catered and fully guided tour.

■ Sonoma Valley Picnic Shopping

From the forested Kenwood area in the north to the open, windswept hills of the Los Carneros area, Sonoma Valley is home to numerous groceries, markets, delis and farm markets. We'll start up north at Kenwood and recommend picnic shopping stops by area where you can put together a meal to suit the delicious East County wines.

> **Kenwood Village Market**
> 8910 State Highway 12
> Kenwood
> 707-833-4801

One-stop economy. Basic deli sandwiches and salads.

Glen Ellen Village Market

13751 Arnold Drive
Glen Ellen
707-996-6728

One stop economy plus fresh produce, deli and good take-away choices for picnics. This is your best stop for Jack London State Park and Benziger Family Winery picnic fare.

SONOMA TOWN

Sonoma Valley Farm Market

Fridays year round from 9 a.m. until noon at Arnold Field in Depot Park, one block and a little bit north of the Sonoma Plaza, downtown Sonoma. There's also an evening market on the Plaza every Tuesday at 5:30 p.m. until dusk, April through October.

A great place to shop for your picnic.

Sonoma Market

520 W. Napa Street
Sonoma
707-996-3411

Five blocks west of the Plaza, this is our choice in town for one-stop economy and deli with nice cheese, seafood and meat department. They also have fresh cooked crabs in season!

Down to Earth Natural Market

201 West Napa Street (in the Sonoma Marketplace)
Sonoma
707-996-9898

Organic products, produce, deli, health and body care.

Lo Spuntino (An Italian Taste of Sonoma)

400 First Street (on the Plaza)

Sonoma

707-935-5656

One-stop deluxe, eat in or take out. A great place for picnic fare! Pastas, salads, panini, rotisserie, gelato, plus delicious Viansa wines and live music schedule. Call for music details.

Sonoma Cheese Factory

2 Spain Street (on the Plaza)

Sonoma

707-996-1931 or 1-800-535-2855

www.sonomacheese.com

Handy on the Plaza. Great picnic fare, deli, and cheese, cheese, cheese. Eat in or take away. Watch the cheese makers at work while your sandwich is made.

Vella Cheese Company

315 Second Street

Sonoma

"It's a factory, not a boutique!" A pleasant stroll south and east of the Plaza will reward your steps with a visit to a Sonoma Valley time warp. Slip into Vella's tiny sales room and back to an era when people bought cheese by the pound or the wheel. No fussy this or that, no cheese sliced to order.

You get to see the cheese makers at work if you take the tour Monday through Thursday at 12:30 p.m. Sample their world-class product and then purchase a hunk of it at the source. We love what goes on inside this find old stone building. Our favorite choice is a great aged Sonoma dry Jack which we use as you would a parmesan cheese from Italy, shaved on salads, on pasta, or nibbled with crisp apples and pears. Yum!

Italian Marketplace at Viansa Winery

25200 Arnold Drive (Carneros Highway 12)

Sonoma

This is the place for your Los Carneros area picnic shopping. The kitchens here turn out inspired picnic fare. Viansa is our first stop shopping suggestion if you're coming up from the Bay Area. It's your last stop as you come down Sonoma Valley from the north, and whichever way you're going, it s a great place for a first-class California taste of Italy. (See page 118.)

GREAT EAST COUNTY PICNIC PLACES

■ Wineries and Roadside Stops

History comes alive in the East County. Sonoma Valley is the birthplace of the California wine industry, site of the northernmost outpost in a string of 21 Franciscan missions, and former seat of the independent Republic of California, an ad hoc government that lasted just 25 days in 1846. You'll also find three state historic parks, two of the oldest wineries in California, a number of museums, and 13,000 acres of world famous vineyards to explore. We'll list a selection of our favorite places by area, starting in the north at Kenwood.

Landmark Vineyards
101 Adobe Canyon Road
Kenwood
707-833-0053

Generally our first stop at the top of the Sonoma Valley, Landmark is a perfect setting for a picnic with Chardonnay in mind. Maple and walnut trees shade the picnic grounds by the pond, and a great splashing fountain and bocce court complete the picture. We particularly enjoy their reasonably priced Adobe Canyon Chardonnay and Claret to accompany simple picnic fare or to take up the road for picnics at Sugarloaf Ridge State Park.

Sugarloaf Ridge State Park

Just five miles up Adobe Canyon Road from Highway 12 and Landmark Vineyards, the quiet canyon picnic sites by Sonoma Creek are shaded and cozy, with plenty of birds, quail, woodpeckers and jays. These tables are just the ticket after a sunny day hike up Bald Mountain Trail for the spectacular view, 5⅜ miles round trip. The park also has a great campground.

Chateau St. Jean

8555 State Highway 12
Kenwood
707-833-4134

Picnic under the pines, redwoods, fragrant cedars, a mighty magnolia, or palms. Tasty wines, exemplary hospitality, a grand historic chateau, and the self-guided winery tour combine to make Chateau St. Jean one of our regular stops.

Warm Springs Road cut-off to Glen Ellen and Arnold Drive

We like to take this back road to the village of Glen Ellen. When you turn off State Highway 12 on Warm Springs Road, you pass through the community of Kenwood. The plaza park with picnic tables provides a pleasant place to stop.

Morton's Warm Springs Park

1651 Warm Springs Road
Kenwood
707-833-5511

The sign on the front gate states: "Cut-offs as swimwear must be double hemmed and clean." I'll bet you a nickel that they check very closely here at Morton's Warm Springs!

A family tradition since the 1930s, this private park is a quaint throwback of sorts. Four to six bucks a head (depending on age and day of the week) will gain you access to the three sparkling pools, picnic tables, barbecues, horseshoe pits and bocce court. You bring the burgers and hot dogs. Pick up a slug of potato salad at the Kenwood Village Market. Whip up a batch of picnic lemonade, and enjoy all the squeals of delight, the yuk, yuk, yuk of the family at the next table (they pack 'em in pretty close at Morton's).

Go ahead, put an ice cube down your sweetheart's swimsuit, goose somebody, wiggle your ears, but no running by the pools, no glass containers, no cannon balls. A little goofing around is OK, but they truck no serious violation of the rules or: "You're out of the pool, bub!"

Jack London State Historic Park
2400 London Ranch Road
Glen Ellen
707-938-5216

Welcome to Jack and Charmian's place. Come see for yourselves. This place, thoughtfully preserved and maintained by volunteers and the State of California, reveals itself personally. Discover a museum, a tomb, a relic, a pond, and the wonderfully diverse flora of Jack London State Historic Park.

After the crowds of summer and harvest, the sun rises later and later, popping up farther each day to the south. Old Sol hurries on his way, casting long fall shadows, but rewarding us in these parts with a particular Mediterranean quality of light and spectacular sunsets. You'll find great beauty at the foot of the Sonoma Mountains. We like to visit in the days before the rains set in. It's Beauty with a capital B, Beauty with a hint of wood smoke. The madrone and oak stacked and dry, the piles of leaves to kick through along the trails—it's the Beauty Ranch.

Break bread, spill some wine to the gods, and picnic with a good book at this grand place of heart in the Valley of the Moon. For further information contact: Valley of the Moon Natural History Association, 2400 London Ranch Road, Glen Ellen, CA 95442.

Benziger Family Winery
1883 London Ranch Road
Glen Ellen
707-935-4046

The Benziger Family invites you to share in the fun of winemaking, fun and family being key ingredients of life on this active Sonoma Mountain Estate. A good portion of the Benziger clan has set up housekeeping on the land they farm. No brutal commute for these folks, they like to be close to the action! Sharing is another key element in the Benziger family business mix. Your visit is well rewarded with an amusing and educational gift of history, art, winemaking and grape growing information, not to mention great wines and lovely terraced picnic grounds.

Sonoma Valley Regional Park
13630 State Highway 12 (four miles south of Kenwood)
707-527-2041

Particularly beautiful in the spring with vibrant green grass and a wealth of wildflowers, this 162-acre park has pleasant oak-shaded picnic areas with barbecue grills and good wheelchair access.

■ The Historic Sonoma Plaza/ Sonoma Area

Classic early California town planning, a thriving community of businesses, museums and historic buildings, Sonoma town is a day's adventure in itself! As your first stop we recommend the helpful **Sonoma Valley Visitors Bureau** at 453 First Street East in the Plaza. Pick up a copy of their handy Visitors Guide.

Stroll the Plaza, visit the cheese factories, put a tasty picnic together, shop for a good used book, and choose a spot to enjoy your meal.

SONOMA PLAZA

Sonoma Plaza is right in the center of town, eight acres in size, and laid out in 1835 by General Vallejo himself. There is a pond, ducks, chickens, and a grand old stone City Hall. The Plaza is picnic central in Sonoma, with tables, acres of shaded lawn, swings for the kids (of all ages) and clean public restrooms located under the offices of the Sonoma Valley Visitors Bureau.

Parking is best at the Vallejo Home State Historic Park, behind the barracks downtown, north of the Plaza, or at Sebastiani Winery where you can pick up a delicious wine and picnic, or hike or bike back up the path.

If you prefer a quieter in-town picnic spot, walk one block (and a little bit) north of the Plaza to **Depot Park**. From Depot Park you can get on the biking/hiking path or check out Arnold Field for hometown sports. Depot Park has barbecue grills, shaded tables, and is home turf to the lively **Valley of the Moon Pètanque Club.**

Explore the **Sonoma biking/hiking path**: A quiet neighborhood north of Spain Street (about 1½ blocks north of the Sonoma Plaza) is blessed with a popular biking/hiking path that runs two miles from Highway 12, past the Vallejo Home "Lachryma Montis," and through Depot Park to Lovall Valley Road and the **Sebastiani Winery** tasting room and picnic grounds.

One of the highlights of Depot Park, pètanque, like bocce, is an outdoor bowling game that has evolved over the millennia from ancient Greek and Roman games. Unlike bocce, Pètanque developed in France, not Italy. If you've ever traveled from Paris to Rome, you might understand the subtle differences and a certain fanaticism attached to these activities that have descended along national lines from what amounts to a bunch of people throwing rocks for sport.

The most obvious difference between the games, whose rules and objectives are virtually identical, is that bocce requires a prepared surface in a defined court or lane, whereas pètanque is played on any unprepared surface of crushed stone or gravel. The French take a more laissez faire approach and you might say that pètanque is the "off road" version of the same game, bocce in four-wheel drive. Beyond the differences between the games, the most obvious similarity is food and wine—food and wine and fun. These games are quintessential picnic pastimes, and a great way to make new friends. We highly recommend you join in on your travels through the wine country. The good folks of the **Valley of the Moon Pètanque Club** host a great casual get-together every fourth Sunday of the month (April or May until November) at Depot Park in Sonoma. Picnic and pètanque, they call it, and they will have the 12-foot rammed earth barbecue fired up, so bring your favorite food, a bottle of wine and join in the fun.

For more information on this event and the Wednesday and Saturday open play season, contact the club at 707-258-3450. The pètanque grounds and barbecue pit are also available for your event or party by reservation.

THE STATE HISTORIC PARK OF SONOMA TOWN

The Sonoma State Historic Park includes the crème de la crème of old California historical treasures: Lachryma Montis, the home of General and Mrs. Mariano Vallejo, the Mission on the Plaza, the remains of the General's "Casa Grande" and the old barracks, also on the Plaza.

A single $2.00 admission fee is good for all locations, and a tour of these old places will give you a good sense of the role of the Sonoma Valley in the days of change preceding the California Gold Rush and the ultimate Americanization of the former Alta California, itself the former lands of numerous native American tribes. For more information call 707-938-1519.

Hello & Goodbye—
The Mission San Francisco Solano in the Sonoma Valley

At a site a few miles south of the present Sonoma Mission (currently the home of Cline Cellars at 24737 State Highway 121) in a valley with a mild climate and permanent springs of sweet water, an ambitious young Franciscan priest set up a temporary alter, and with a volley of gunfire from the accompanying Mexican soldiers, celebrated the first Mass of his new mission in Sonoma Valley on July 4, 1823.

The irony of this religious gunplay was probably not lost on the local Coast Miwoks who by this date were already way familiar with this church-state, war pony-and-dogma show from the sad experiences of their neighbors to the south.

The traditional Coast Miwok tenure in the pleasant valley was all but over. The new folks, the Franciscans of the Roman Catholic Church, acting in disharmonious concert with the fledgling Mexican government, would virtually enslave the Miwoks for their own purposes. Local Indian labor would, among other things, build some of the very buildings that now compose the Sonoma Historic District.

The policies and politics of three expansionist world powers (Mexico, Russia and the United States) would, in the years following the establishment of the Mission, so trivialize the existence of the indigenous peoples that those who survived were rounded up and sent to live with the remnants of neighboring tribes in the agriculturally marginal areas to the north in Lake and Mendocino Counties . . . Hello, and Goodbye!

~~~

HELLO AGAIN!

If you would like to learn more about the Coast Miwok way of life, we recommend you visit **Kule Loklo**, a Coast Miwok cultural exhibit at the Bear

Valley Visitor Center in **Point Reyes National Seashore**. The Visitor Center is located off of Bear Valley Road, just about a mile north and west of the town of Olema in Marin County.

Kule Loklo is a replica of a typical Coast Miwok village, and we can imagine it shares many similarities with the community set-up of their immediate neighbors, the Pomo and Wappo peoples who inhabited Mendocino and Sonoma counties in pre-European contact times. You might want to call ahead for a schedule of events and interpretive walks.

Point Reyes National Seashore Visitors Center

Point Reyes
415-663-1092
The rangers and staff of the Point Reyes National Seashore welcome your questions on the traditional Native American ways and life.

Sebastiani Sonoma Cask Cellars

389 Fourth Street East
Sonoma
707-938-5532
Busy, friendly and fun! Enjoy the wines and a tour, then take a walk on the bike path through Depot Park, or enjoy a picnic under the olive trees.

Ravenswood

18701 Gehricke Road
Sonoma
707-938-1960
www.ravenswood-wine.com
For a pleasant picnic with robust red wine in mind, visit our friends at Ravenswood. From Sebastiani (at 4th and Lovall Valley Road), walk or bike ride out Lovall Valley Road to Gehricke Road. Follow the signs to the winery and enjoy "big, gutsy, unapologetic wines" and the company of Clackamas, the big, mellow winery cat.

Bartholomew Park Winery
1000 Vineyard Lane
Sonoma, CA 95476
707-935-9511
www.bartholomewparkwinery.com

Only a 1⅜-mile hike from Sebastiani (at 4th and Lovall Valley Road), follow the signs to an extraordinary winery. We would like to share just enough information on this gem of an operation to cause you to wander up Vineyard Lane and see for yourself. Superb hand-crafted wine for starters, an exceptional setting with the best picnic grounds in the East County, and three miles of hiking trails should be reason enough to pique your interest, but there is more. I particularly enjoy the wall of portraits of all the growers, the faces behind the vines who provide the grapes. You'll also find a museum, a cheery staff, the winery cats, a welcoming winemaker who favors an organic approach to his craft, and a chance to see a big pileated woodpecker that calls this great place home.

Buena Vista Winery
1800 Old Winery Road
Sonoma
1-800-926-1266

California's oldest premium winery with a shaded creekside picnic area, Buena Vista is rich in history and fine old stonework, plus delicious wines.

Gundlach-Bundschu Winery
2000 Denmark Street
Vineburg
707-938-5277
www.gunbun.com

Six generations of hands-on, spirited growing and winemaking show up in every bottle produced here on the 400-acre Rhinefarm. This is a fun place, and a favorite stop for an amusing picnic—check out their posters, for example. If you arrive in early spring, you might catch the frog hatch. A world of peepers in the frog pond all singing and crazed with their seasonal imperative.

Cline Cellars
24737 State Highway 121
Sonoma, CA 95476
707-935-4310
www.clinecellars.com

Tasty Rhone-style wines and a tranquil picnic grounds keep us coming back to Cline Cellars.

Viansa Winery and Italian Marketplace
25200 State Highway 121
Sonoma, CA 95476
707-935-4700
www.viansa.com

Like a grand renaissance cathedral fashioned by the hand of man to focus one's mind on the glories of heaven, the Viansa Winery and Italian Marketplace is raised up in exaltation of the wine country picnic. The wines, the food, the setting with a view, this place is designed to enrapture.

A sunny late summer day is a good time to visit, to take in the miles of rolling hills, the terraced vineyards and golden grass. But we like winter visits too when the wetlands are full with the season's rain. We bring binoculars to watch the ducks while eating olives, lost in our vagabond dreams of Tuscany.

■ Dining Out in the East County

After a day of East County picnicking, wine tasting and hiking, we almost always finish with a browse through the bookstores and shops on the Sonoma Plaza. Due in large part to the effects of the aroma of good cooking that drifts around the Plaza as the evening specials are coming out of the ovens and broilers, we tend to follow our noses to a light meal at one of our favorite bars.

The Swiss Hotel (Since 1909)
18 W. Spain Street
Sonoma, CA 95476
707-938-2884
Cozy, cheerful, great wood-oven pizza, we love the tiny bar at the old Swiss Hotel. They also have a pleasant dining room and patio, plus five popular rooms for overnight guests. Reserve a room well in advance.

Murphy's Irish Pub
464 First Street East
Sonoma, CA 95476
707-935-0660
Sometimes after a full day on the wine roads, you just feel like having a world-class pint and a plate of fish and chips. It happens. Also, great live music!

Piatti Ristorante at the El Dorado Hotel
405 First Street West
Sonoma, CA 95476
707-996-2351
Lively atmosphere and good cooking. We enjoy a light supper at the friendly bar.

■ After Dinner

We like to wander around the Plaza, catch some Irish music at **Murphy's** and local chat at the venerable **Stieners**, or coffee in the garden at **The Coffee Garden**. If you fancy some blues, we highly recommend a drive out to 17154 Highway 12 and the **Valley of the Moon Saloon** in Fetters Hot Springs. Call for a music schedule: 707-996-4003.

9
Activities & Diversions

Best Places to Browse and Shop

■ West County

HEALDSBURG

Healdsburg has great thrift shopping, a good way to put together or augment your picnic gear. Need a pepper mill?

St. John's Used Treasure Shoppe
201 Center Street
707-433-8533

Goodwill Store
513 Healdsburg Avenue
707-431-8408

Salvation Army Thrift Store
200 Lytton Springs Road
707-433-7404

A gorgeous setting for a thrift shop! Three miles out of town, north on Highway 101 to Lytton Springs exit, go west .25 mile to this extraordinary complex.

◆

Of course West Sonoma County's towns, both large and small, offer many other great shopping opportunities, but we'll let you discover them on your own. You might explore the distinctive downtowns of Sebastopol, Petaluma, Guerneville, and tiny Graton, plus Railroad Square in Santa Rosa.

In the East County we particulary recommend **Sonoma Plaza** in downtown Sonoma and **Jack London Village** on Arnold Drive south of Glen Ellen.

■ Sonoma County Book Shops

HEALDSBURG PLAZA

Levin & Company
306 Center Street
707-433-1118
New and used books, great jazz music selection.

Toyon Books
104 Matheson Street
707-433-9270
New books on the Plaza.

Pratum Book Company
314 Center Street
707-431-2634
www.pratum.com
Antiquarian and scholarly books by appointment or catalogue only.

WEST COUNTY

Black Bart Books
25200 Highway 116
Duncans Mills
707-869-9520

Cold Mountain Books
9050 Graton Road
Graton
707-823-2881

Copperfield's Books and Music
www.copperfld.com
650 4th Street, Santa Rosa: 707-545-5326
New and used books, cafe.

2316 Montgomery Drive, Montgomery Village, Santa Rosa: 707-578-8938
New books and music.

210 Coddingtown Center, Santa Rosa: 707-575-0550
New books.

138 N. Main Street, Sebastopol: 829-0429 (used), 823-2618 (new)
New and used books, music, cafe.

140 Kentucky St., Petaluma: 707-782-0228 (used), 762-0563 (new)
New and used books, cafe.

Treehorn Books
625 4th Street
Santa Rosa
707-525-1782
New, used and out-of-print books.

North Light Books
530 E. Cotati Avenue
Cotati
707-792-4300

Twice Told Books
14045 Armstrong Woods Road
Guerneville
707-869-1479
Used books.

River Reader
16355 Main Street
Guerneville
707-869-2240
New books.

EAST COUNTY

Jack London Bookstore
14300 Arnold Drive
Glen Ellen
707-996-2888
An unusual collection of used books with a great

range of books by and about Jack London and the west.

Sonoma Plaza is a great book lovers destination.

Book Nook
414 First Street, Suite F (El Paseo Courtyard)
Sonoma Plaza
707-938-3280
Used paperbacks.

Chanticleer Books
526 Broadway
Sonoma
707-996-5364
chantbks@vom.com
Used and rare books.

Plaza Books
40 W. Spain Street
Sonoma
707-996-8474
plazabks@sonic.com
www.plazabooks.com
Food, wine, western Americana, antiquarian.

Pyramid Books
11 East Napa Street
Sonoma
707-996-1460

Reader's Books
127 East Napa Street
Sonoma
707-939-1779
New books.

Sonoma Bookends
201 W. Napa Street, #18 Sonoma Marketplace
Sonoma
707-938-5926
New books.

POINT REYES STATION, WEST MARIN

Brown Study Bookshop
415-663-1633
New and used books.

Manfred's
415-663-9646
New and used books.

■ A Special Attraction

Safari West
3115 Porter Creek Road
Santa Rosa
707-579-2551
www.safariwest.com
This privately owned and operated ranch in the hills between Santa Rosa and Calistoga 15 minutes off Highway 101 is a haven for an amazing collection of African animals and birds. To plan a visit, arrange for lodging in a cozy tent cabin, or inquire about holding an event, contact Peter or Nancy Lang.

■ Favorite Pubs, Lounges and Hideaways

We have always been intrigued by funky little out-of-the-way watering holes. Since January 1, 1998, all California public establishments have been declared non-smoking, so now it's easier to enjoy these cozy small businesses.

Catelli's "The Rex"
241 Healdsburg Avenue
Healdsburg
707-433-6000
Where the growers meet and greet—great bar, local wines, Italian lunch and dinner.

John & Zeke's
111 Plaza Street
Healdsburg
707-433-3735
A friendly local bar with pool and shuffleboard.

Felix & Louie's
106 Matheson
Healdsburg
707-433-6966
Wood-fired pizza oven and full bar.

The Bar at the Dry Creek Store
3495 Dry Creek Road
In Dry Creek Valley
707-431-1543
A no-frills country tavern; extra friendly with a hideaway deck for sunset brews.

George's Hideaway
18100 Highway 116
Two miles west of Guerneville
Classic turn-of-the-century roadhouse. Check out the bar, carved in 1954 by two ladies who traded the work for their tab. Best fireplace, home cooking and lively dice games.

Pink Elephant
9895 Main Street
Monte Rio
707-865-0500
The town of Monte Rio, a little rough around the edges lately, is the classic Russian River resort community. You get the feeling that the place was really swinging back in the 1930s, '40s and '50s! Dodge in here and check out the collection of elephant kitsch

and the hysterically historical painting behind the bar.

Blue Heron Restaurant & Tavern
1 Steelhead Blvd.
Duncans Mills
707-865-9135
This place gets points for food and atmosphere! Have a little cruise about the town of Duncans Mills, population 85, then try the Blue Heron for a bite and a brew.

River's End
11051 Highway 1 at Jenner
707-865-2484
A pleasant bar with a spectacular view of the Russian River mouth. Good cooking and lodging too!

Union Saloon at the Union Hotel
3731 Main Street
Occidental
707-874-3555
An historic old watering hole, circa 1879.

Washoe House
Four miles north of Petaluma on Stony Point Road at the corner of Roblar Road
707-795-4544
Full bar, lunch and dinner
We enjoy stopping at this historic public house, which started in 1859 as a stop on the Petaluma-Santa Rosa stage line. It's the oldest place of its kind in the county and serves good food and beverages.

Casino
17150 Bodega Highway
Bodega
707-876-3185
A favorite stop. See page 81.

William Tell House Restaurant and Bar
26955 Highway 1
Tomales
707-878-2403
Circa 1877—very historic. Lunch, dinner and cozy bar.

Nick's Cove
On Highway 1, three miles north of the town
of Marshall on Tomales Bay
415-663-1033
*A classically coastal family-owned and operated
bar and seafood house.*

Western Saloon
11201 State Route 1
Point Reyes Station
*One of the few places where patrons still arrive
on horseback. Knock one down with the cowfolk!*

Vladimir's
On Sir Francis Drake Blvd.
Downtown Inverness
415-669-1021
*Vladimir does most all the cooking now, and the
service, too, so don't expect the full menu on any given
day. As a matter of fact, don't expect that he will even
be there at all, what with the skiing, the horseback
riding, the rewards of a life lived well. Do go through
the door, if it happens to be open, and be open to a place
where change can happen (see story below).*

The Simple Twists of Fate

*It was an evening to remember, mid-July, 1970. Things
can happen that change your life, just a simple twist
of fate. I walked in through Vladimir's door and when
I came out, things were different. I used to work in the
mills and factories back east, but now I'm a cook by
trade and living in California.*

*Was it the homemade bread, dense and chewy? Was
it the Petaluma duck, roasted crisp with a side of sweet
and sour red cabbage and a tall, cold, glass of beer?
The dumplings? Maybe it was the no-nonsense guy in
the tall riding boots, jodhpurs and apron, or the
affectionate rapport he had with his wife who was
cooking in the back of this old house of a tavern. It
might have been the lively chatter and small town
banter at the bar, or the raucous table of longhairs,*

wind-burnt high from a day's sailing on Tomales Bay.

California dreaming had gotten a good hold on me around the tail end of the 1960s. The very day after I was released from a thirteen-year sentence in the Michigan Public Schools, my young thumb was out and I was west coast bound. Up and over the Mackinaw Bridge, goodbye Detroit, west on U.S. Highway 2, beer-soaked in Wisconsin and snowed on in Montana. Down through Idaho and Utah, to bob like a cork in the Great Salt Lake. Shake that cloak of winter, the union job, the grind of the line.

The surf was up at Malibu, but skinny and frost-bound-midnight-pale, I didn't make the scene. San Francisco seemed more the place for me, so I hooked up with my father and his $255 Ford Falcon. We put southern California behind us for a week and headed north on Highway 1.

Dad had gotten the jump on me in December of 1969, while I was still locked down in high school with a swing-shift work release in a miserable rat hole of a die cast shop. I saved every penny and prayed for spring. Dad was having a little holiday from his regular life as a steady workaday bread winner and had left the wife and kids behind in Michigan to build a new life for the family in sunny California.

Dad used to tell great stories about California. He had passed through on his way to and from the agony of the Philippines in 1942 and 1945. He was on top of his game in those days, and it was always with a long sigh and the far away look that he would lament, "I haven't been to California since the War."

One day, after years of hearing this plaintive line, my mom suggested, "Well, what are you waiting for?" That was his cue and he immediately arranged a two-week vacation for himself in the fabled City of Angels.

Curiously, he returned after only one week with an uncharacteristically grand announcement. "We're moving to California," he said. "Not with two kids still in school and no jobs, we're not," replied my mother, always the stickler for details. Dad left a couple *of weeks later for a job at Whittier College and a room in the Whittier Motel on Whittier Boulevard in Whittier, California.*

That's where I caught up with him. He was sitting in the shade of an old oak tree, enjoying a beer and shooting the breeze with his neighbor, Mr. Gonzales, who spoke very little English but was a loquacious man with his eyeballs, eyebrows, shoulders and fingers. Mr. Gonzales was a janitor at Whittier College, and one day when I paid a visit to the campus, he took me by the arm and pointed out a musty old pair of gym shoes prominently displayed in a glass case full of minor trophies. "The shoes of the President," he said proudly, and I could tell it was a line he had delivered before. Sure enough, I was standing on an immaculately waxed linoleum floor in front of the gym shoes of Richard Milhous Nixon.

Nixon was a Whittier alum, and looking down at my own beat sneakers I couldn't help but wonder how the Honorable Richard Milhous Nixon would feel, standing in my shoes with a bad-news draft number hung on him like a hangman's noose.

My father (God bless his little pointed head) was no Nixon-lover. He told me of a midnight vigil the students had on campus to protest United States involvement in a conflict a half a world away. "Hundreds of kids with candles, and absolutely silent," he said. To witness that spectacle of calm, controlled rage in the days following Kent State gave my old man the materials we needed to build a shaky bridge between us in that time of loss.

Dad and I managed a hell of a good road trip from L.A. to Oxnard and Morro Bay, with shots and beers in Monterey. We made it all the way up to the Point Reyes Lighthouse in our travels and had that wonderful dinner at Vladimir's in Inverness.

■ Cultural Events

Luther Burbank Center for the Arts
50 Mark West Springs Road
(east side of Highway 101)
Santa Rosa
707-546-3600
This venue brings 100 performances a year to the community, with a wide variety of cultural and popular programs. Watch the local papers or call for upcoming shows.

■ Surf Scene

Despite southern California's reputation as Surf City, the north coast offers plenty of decent rides. You'll need a wet suit in these chill waters though. Call or visit the righteous dudes and dudettes at:

Bodega Bay Surf Shack
1400 Highway 1 in Pelican Plaza
Bodega Bay
707-875-3944
www.bodegabaysurf.com

Northern Light Surf Shop
17190 Bodega Highway
Bodega
707-876-3032

■ Windsurfing

The southeast corner of Bodega Harbor seems to be the place to shred, but what do I know? I just like to sit at **The Dog House** with a beer and watch the action. Call the surf shops for excellent advice on windsurfing and conditions.

■ Canoes and Kayaks

Perhaps the most intimate way to see Sonoma County's river and bay shore wildlife is from the water in a human-powered boat. Call these fine establishments for more information and rentals.

> **Blue Waters Kayaking**
> 12938 Sir Francis Drake Blvd.
> Inverness
> 415-669-2600

> **Burke's Russian River Canoe Trips**
> 707-887-1222

> **Tamal Saka**
> **Tomales Bay Kayaking**
> 19225 State Route 1
> Marshall
> 415-663-1743
> *Eco-hip and great tours and instruction.*

■ Ocean Fishing Adventures

See the whales up close, catch your supper, or just enjoy a day on the big water watching the birds and getting a different perspective on the gorgeous coast.

> **Bodega Bay Sport Fishing Center**
> 1500 Bay Flat Road
> Bodega Bay
> 707-875-3344
> *Fishing, bird and whale watching.*

> **Will's Fishing Adventures**
> 1580 East Shore Road
> Bodega Bay
> 707-878-2323
> *Bottom fishing, salmon, albacore and crab.*

■ Abalone Diving

We love to eat them, but we don't know a darned thing about capturing 'em. For the best information, contact a local dive shop, and tune your radio to 91.1 FM, every other Monday night from 8 to 10 p.m. to get dive reports on the Average Abalone show. Local diver Johnny Bazzano spins tunes and dishes dive tips. Call 585-8522 for exact show dates.

Ab season runs April through June and August through November. You're required to have a fishing license, the ab endorsement sticker and a pry bar.

Bodega Bay Pro Dive
1275 Highway 1
Bodega Bay
707-875-3054

■ In the Spirit—Area Churches and Sacred Places

The original inhabitants of this neighborhood held that every thing and place was imbued with spirit, some good and some bad. Sacred places, though lost to the map makers and guide book writers, are still to be found in the personal experiences of the traveler willing to take the time to pause and reflect. A solitary rock, a grand old cluster of oak or pepperwood trees, a pretty turn on a year-round stream, or the prominent bald hill facing a distant unknown over the immense wild sea. Good vibes abound. Sonoma County has countless subtly beautiful spots to stop and give thanks in the great outdoors.

If it's a roof over your head and the fellowship of kindred souls you crave, you'll find a full listing of area churches in local phone books.

■ In Touch—Spa and Massage

Since our area sits at the active juncture of two continental plates, Sonoma and our surrounding counties have several resorts where you can relax in style and enjoy warm mineral waters.

Osmosis Enzyme Bath & Massage
209 Bohemian Highway
Freestone
707-823-8231
Enter through the lovely Japanese garden and find relaxation and serenity in an enzyme bath. Massage and blanket wraps too.

A Bodega Day
Bodega
707-824-9491
Horseback riding, hiking and massage therapy.

A Simple Touch Spa
239 Center Street
Healdsburg
707-433-6856

Spa off the Plaza
706 Healdsburg Avenue
Healdsburg
707-431-7938

Sonoma Mission Inn and Spa
18140 Highway 12
Boyes Hot Springs
707-938-9000
If you really need pampering (and can afford it), try this elegantly restored old resort.

SOAK YOUR WEARY BONES IN NAPA COUNTY

The town of Calistoga sits in the spectacular peak-rimmed northern end of the Napa Valley. It's just over the hills east of Santa Rosa via twisting Petrified Forest or Mark West Springs roads. Calistoga has been famous for their therapeutic springs and spas since the 1800s. Of course native peoples gathered there before then for the healing waters.

Legend has it that Calistoga got its name when Mormon entrepeneurial tycoon Sam Brannan, who had just opened a resort, drunkenly boasted to a boisterous banquet crowd that he'd "turn this town into the Calistoga of Sarifornia," mistakenly attempting to name the famed New York hot springs resort. Call the Calistoga Chamber of Commerce at 707-942-6333 for more information.

MELLOW OUT IN LAKE COUNTY

Harbin Hot Springs Retreat and Workshop Center
Harbin Hot Springs Road
Middletown
800-622-2477
www.harbin.org
Natural springs in a lovely setting. Day visits, massage, camping and lodging.

MENDOCINO COUNTY

Vichy Springs Resort
2605 Vichy Springs Road
Ukiah
707-462-9515

Orr Hot Springs Resort
13201 Orr Springs Road
Ukiah
707-462-6277
Natural springs in a remote canyon. Reservations are required for day use or overnight camping or lodging.

■ Local Radio Guide

FM BAND

KRCB 91.1 FM: Redwood Public Radio
Michele Anna Jordan's Mouthful, local food news and interviews Sundays at 7 p.m. Great local radio and NPR, plus Johnny Bazzano's Average Abalone every other Monday night, 8 to 10 p.m.

KQED 88.5 FM: San Francisco Public Radio *More NPR programming.*

KMGG "Oldies" 97.7 FM

KFGY "Froggy" 92.9 FM: *Country*

KXFX "The Fox" 101.7 FM: *Rock*

KJZY "Jazzy" FM 93.7

AM BAND

KCBS 740 AM: *Traffic, weather and news.*

KGO 810 AM: *Gene Burns' food, wine and travel on Saturdays 10 a.m. to 1 p.m. News talk.*

KRRS 1460 AM: *La Maquina Musical/Regional Mexican.*

KSRO 1350 AM: *News and talk plus John Ash and Steve Garner's Good Food Hour every Saturday morning, 11 a.m. until noon.*

■ Calendar of Events

Please call for dates and details.

JANUARY

A year in the wine country starts with pruning of the vines. Look for the pruning crews in their yellow rain slickers working their way through the rows.

Russian River Winter Wineland
707-586-3795
A weekend of tasting and education.

The ZAP Tasting
530-274-4900
Annual Zinfandel barrel tasting at Fort Mason Center in San Francisco.

Old-Time Fiddle Contest
Cloverdale Citrus Fairgrounds, 707-894-3992

FEBRUARY

The daffodils and acacia are in bloom and pruning continues.

Winter Wine and Food Series
707-586-3795

Citrus Fair
Cloverdale Citrus Fairgrounds, 707-894-3992

MARCH

New green grass spreads over the hills, the tulips come out, and the vines begin to awaken.

Russian River Wine Road Barrel Tasting
707-586-3795

Heart of the Valley Barrel Tasting
Kenwood Area Wineries, 707-833-5891

Sonoma County Folk Festival
Luther Burbank Center for the Arts
Santa Rosa, 707-546-3600

Prime whale watching *on the coast as the northbound migration starts.*

APRIL

"Bud break"—everyone looks forward to the first green on the vines as winter gives way to spring. The crews you see out in the freshly prepared fields are planting root stock for new vineyards. The wild iris and lupine are in bloom.

Spring Thing
Guerneville, 707-869-9000

Fitch Mountain Footrace and Walk
707-433-6935

Fisherman Festival
Bodega Bay, 707-875-3422
Bathtub races and the blessing of the fleet.

Historic Home Tour
Healdsburg, 707-433-6935

Sebastopol Apple Blossom Festival
707-823-3032

April in Carneros Open House Weekend
Carneros Area Wineries, 707-939-9363

MAY

The vineyards are lush with new growth. The crews are out thinning the leaves and training the vines to the wires of the trellising system.

Russian River Women's Weekend #1
Guerneville, 707-869-9000

Future Farmers Country Fair and Twilight Parade
Healdsburg, 707-433-6935

Memorial Day Weekend Antique Fair
On the Plaza in Healdsburg, 707-433-6935

Cinco de Mayo Celebration
Sonoma Plaza, 707-938-4626

JUNE

A month of color and warm, long days.

Russian River Blues Festival
Guerneville, 707-869-9000

Russian River Rodeo
Guerneville, 707-869-9000
Parade and barbecue.

Art and Artisan Show
Sonoma Plaza, 707-996-1090

Ox Roast
Sonoma Plaza, 707-996-1090

JULY

The heart of summer—reservations are recommended for everything, a time when picnicking really pays off. You might see the vineyard crews cutting fruit from the vines and tossing it onto the ground. This baffled us our first season in wine country. It's called thinning, and though seemingly wasteful, it's an essential movement to the farmer's dance for it isn't the amount of fruit on the vine, but the quality of the fruit that counts. Thinning helps concentrate flavors in the remaining grapes.

Fourth of July Fireworks:

Healdsburg: 707-433-6935
Guerneville: 707-869-9000
Cloverdale: 707-894-4470
Bodega Bay: 707-875-3422
Sonoma Town: 707-996-1090

World Pillow Fighting Championships
707-833-2440
Loads of fun in Plaza Park, Kenwood.

Healdsburg Harvest Century Bike Tour
800-648-9922

Sonoma County Fair
Fairgrounds, Santa Rosa, 707-545-4200

Living History Day at Fort Ross State Historic Park
707-847-3286

Sunday Concerts in the Plaza
Healdsburg, 707-433-6935

Sonoma County Showcase and Wine Auction
 800-939-7666
A wonderful, fun event to benefit the Boys and Girls Club.

AUGUST

The month of wait-and-see—cellar crews are busy preparing tanks and barrels for the coming crush.

From Grape to Glass Tastings
707-546-3276

Healdsburg Guitar Festival
Villa Chanticleer, 707-433-6935/800-648-9922

Street Dance on Healdsburg Avenue
Healdsburg, 707-433-6935

Healdsburg Farmers Market Zucchini Festival
707-433-6935

Accordion Festival
Cotati, 707-664-0444
Polka dance party in La Plaza Park.

Sunday Concerts in the Plaza
Healdsburg, 707-433-6935

Bodega Bay Seafood, Art and Wine Festival
707-875-2721

Old Adobe Festival
Petaluma Adobe State Historic Park
Petaluma, 707-762-4871
Square dancing and Native American dance.

Wine Country Film Festival
Sonoma, 707-996-2536

SEPTEMBER

Harvest—from late August to early October, experience the full-tilt excitement of the harvest. Norteño, Mariachi, or Tejano music blasts from the the boom boxes accor-

ding to each crew's tastes. The pickers race with lugs of fruit held overhead to the bins where the foreman records their tally. Everyone's on the run. It's the focal point of our year.

Silver salmon season *begins for offshore fishing and the Russian River.*

Harbor Seal Watch
At the mouth of the Russian River
Jenner, 707-875-3422

Russian River Jazz Festival
Guerneville, 707-869-9000

Valley of the Moon Vintage Festival
Downtown Sonoma, 707-996-2109
Blessing of the grapes in Sonoma Plaza.

Labor Day Weekend Antique Fair
On the Plaza in Healdsburg, 707-433-6935

Women's Weekend #2
Guerneville, 707-869-9000

OCTOBER

Gorgeous colors adorn the hills, roses bloom everywhere and the first frost hits.

Sonoma County Harvest Fair
Santa Rosa, 707-545-4203

NOVEMBER

Rain and sleep for the vines, olive harvest begins, and everyone joins in thanksgiving for the fruits of the season.

Steelhead season begins *for the Russian River.*

North Bay Veterans Day Parade
Downtown Petaluma, 707-762-0591
The real deal—a day for those who answered the call.

DECEMBER

Olive harvest continues. The vines sleep while the field crews prune away the summer's canes.

Healdsburg Antique Dealers Open House
707-433-6935

Historic Tree Walk
Downtown Healdsburg, 707-431-3301

Christmas at the Sonoma Mission
707-938-1519

Gray whale migration *reaches its southbound peak in mid-month.*

10

Heading In/Heading Out

A visit to Sonoma County fits neatly with a stop in the San Francisco Bay Area or one of our other neighboring counties. A list of helpful phone numbers follows. Please refer to **Appendix C: Resoures** for more information.

■ San Francisco and the Bay Area

The City, Baghdad by the Bay (please don't call it Frisco)—however you refer to this gem of a town, a good place to start your research or explorations is a copy of the San Francisco Chronicle. Sunday editions are available at news stands in most cities nationwide, or visit the Chronicle on the Web at www.sfgate.com. You might also try:

> **San Francisco Visitor's Center**
> 415-391-2000
> www.sfvisitor.org
>
> **Oakland Convention Center**
> 800-262-5526

■ Marin County

This guide provides information on a small corner of Marin County, namely the Tomales Bay and Point Reyes Station area. For more information on Marin County call:

> **Marin County Convention and Visitor's Bureau:** 415-472-7470
>
> **San Rafael Chamber of Commerce**
> 415-454-4163

■ Mendocino County

Directly north of Sonoma County, Mendocino County is similar in many respects, but with far less population. Being farther from northern California's main urban centers means more quiet and open spaces. For information call:

>**Fort Bragg-Mendocino Coast Chamber of Commerce:** 707-961-6300
>
>**Ukiah Chamber of Commerce**
>707-462-4705
>
>**Willits Chamber of Commerce**
>707-459-7910

■ Lake County

For information about our other northern neighbor and the Clear Lake area call:

>**Greater Lakeport Chamber of Commerce**
>707-263-5092

■ Napa County

For information on Napa Valley and vicinity, we suggest you contact the following Chambers of Commerce:

>**City of Napa:** 707-226-7455
>**St. Helena:** 707-963-4456
>**Calistoga:** 707-942-6333

■ Sonoma County

For more information on Sonoma County, contact these helpful offices:

California Welcome Center and Sonoma County Winery Association
5000 Roberts Lake Drive, Rohnert Park
707-586-3795
Located just off Highway 101 at the Golf Course Drive Exit in Rohnert Park.

Sonoma County Convention and Visitors Bureau
5000 Roberts Lake Drive, Rohnert Park
707-586-8100

Sonoma Valley Visitors Bureau
20 E. Spain, Sonoma
707-996-1090

Sonoma Valley Chamber of Commerce
651-A Broadway, Sonoma
707-996-1033

Sebastopol Chamber of Commerce
265 S. Main, Sebastopol
707-823-3032

Petaluma Chamber of Commerce
799 Baywood Drive, Suite #3, Petaluma
707-762-2785

■ APPENDIX A: Getting Here/ Mode of Travel

The following is a basic rundown on ways to reach Sonoma County and a list of helpful phone numbers and addresses. For more information on the Bay Area and neighboring counties, refer to **Chapter 10: Heading In/Heading Out** and **Appendix C: Resources.**

AIR TRAVEL

Two major airports serve our corner of northern California: **San Francisco International Airport** (650-876-2377) and **Oakland International Airport** (510-577-4000). Most major airlines serve San Francisco, Oakland or both terminals.

For connecting air service from San Francisco International Airport to the smaller Sonoma County Airport, a very scenic 30-minute hop, call **United Airlines** at 800-241-6522 and press option #3, or ask for United Express service to Sonoma County Airport. For auto rental at Sonoma County Airport, you can arrange to have a car waiting for you by calling **Hertz** at 800-654-3131. Ask for Santa Rosa, California at the Sonoma County Airport.

For bus shuttle service to Sonoma County from San Francisco International Airport, call the **Santa Rosa Airporter** at 707-545-8015, or **Sonoma County Airport Express** at 707-837-8700. For other auto rental options in the Santa Rosa area, contact **Freeman Toyota** at 800-225-3055, **Hansel Ford** at 707-526-1650, or **Enterprise Rent-a-Car** at 800-325-8007. For shuttle service from San Francisco International Airport to San Francisco locations, call **Supershuttle** at 415-659-2547.

TRAVEL BY CAR OR MOTORCYCLE

The most convenient way but by no means the only way to get around is by car or motorcycle. If you haven't brought your own, or are tagging along with friends or relatives, here's the scoop on vehicle rental.

All the major car rental companies will be happy to help you with auto rentals at San Francisco or Oakland Airports. For a more exotic means of travel during the dry season, ideal for folks with adventuresome spirits and two-wheel skills, you might try the following for motorcycle rentals.

Eaglerider American Classic Rentals
1555 Burke Avenue, Unit 0
San Francisco, 888-390-4600

Rent a Harley in San Rafael
777 E. Francisco Blvd.
San Rafael, CA 94901, 415-927-4464

FOOT TRAVEL/PUBLIC TRANSPORTATION

Admittedly not the most convenient, public transit and even walking can be workable ways to see the world if you plan ahead, have some extra time, and will be visiting Sonoma County during our extended dry season. We're acquainted with the heroics of foot travel in winter by the very young-of-heart or desperate from our own young and desperate pasts. We suggest you arrange a place to stay, explore that area, then move on to another base location. Good base locations might be Healdsburg, Guerneville, Occidental, Bodega Bay or the town of Sonoma.

Golden Gate Transit, 415-923-2000, provides bus service between San Francisco and Santa Rosa Transit Mall. Route #80 goes from San Francisco to Santa Rosa. Board at the corner of First and Mission Streets in San Francisco.

Sonoma County Transit, 707-576-7433, provides bus service in our area of interest. The service is limited, so planning ahead is essential for the foot traveler. We recommend you call during business hours, Monday through Friday, or write for schedule information (355 W. Robles Avenue, Santa Rosa, CA 95407).

The main bus routes connect with the Transit

Mall in downtown Santa Rosa and serve the following areas:

#62 – Sonoma County Airport

#60 – Healdsburg, Geyserville, and Cloverdale on Highway 101

#20 – Forestville, Guerneville and Occidental

For bus service from the Santa Rosa Transit Mall to the coast, call **Mendocino Transit Authority** (MTA) at 800-696-4682. Their Santa Rosa/Point Arena Route #95 provides daily service to Bodega Bay, Jenner, Fort Ross and points north.

You may also get to the Point Reyes Station, Tomales Bay and National Seashore area on public transportation. **Golden Gate Transit Route #65** runs twice daily Saturdays, Sundays and holidays only from the San Rafael Transit Mall to the town of Inverness. Call 415-455-2000.

TRAIN TRAVEL ON AMTRAK

Yes, people still can and do go by train, although nowadays train travel also can include a shuttle bus ride from the main station in Emeryville, California. Amtrak can be a great way to see the country if you have the time and money; we suggest you book early, and be somewhat flexible about details such as arrival and departure times.

Amtrak Reservations: 1-800-872-7245

It is possible to visit Sonoma County by a train/bus combination, but it's a convoluted process. Here are the basics. Call the good folks at Amtrak for the details.

There are two main lines that serve the Bay Area: **The Coast Starlight** runs between Los Angeles and Seattle. **The California Zephyr** runs between Chicago and Emeryville, just north of Oakland.

Both trains arrive too late to connect with bus #6313 which runs once a day from the Martinez Station to Petaluma on Highway 101 in Sonoma County, and from there heads up Highway 101 to

Santa Rosa, Healdsburg, Cloverdale, Ukiah and points north as far as McKinleyville north of Eureka. Any which way you approach this combination requires a night over in Martinez, or a night in Emeryville, Oakland or San Francisco, plus a shuttle back to Martinez the next day.

I suggest you purchase a ticket to San Francisco (which requires a bus shuttle from the East Bay stations) and rent a car or travel by Golden Gate Transit to the bus mall in Santa Rosa and then on to Sonoma County Transit buses to your final wine country destination . . . whew!

OTHER TRANSPORTATION

By April 2000 (with a little luck), passenger and excursion service will run on the old Northwestern Pacific tracks between Healdsburg and Willits, offering a fun ride on a gorgeous route. For information, call 800-550-2122.

For Sonoma County taxi and limo service, call **A-C Taxi,** 707-526-4888, **George's Taxi,** 707-546-3322, or **Lon's Limo Scene,** 707-539-5466.

Transportation from San Francisco International Airport to the town of Sonoma and vicinity is provided by **Sonoma Airporter,** 707-938-4246, and **California Wine Tours & Transportation,** 707-938-4248.

Public transportation is provided by **Golden Gate Transit,** 415-923-2000, with Monday through Friday service from San Francisco to the Sonoma Valley on Route #90. For weekend service you must catch the San Francisco to Santa Rosa, Route #80 Golden Gate Transit bus to the Santa Rosa Transit Mall.

Sonoma County Transit, 707-576-7433, provides connecting service from Santa Rosa to Sonoma Valley on Route #30. Local Sonoma Valley service is on Route #32. Please call the helpful folks at either of these companies for up to the minute information. Be advised service is quite limited.

Taxi Service is provided by **Bear Flag Taxi,** 707-996-6733.

■ APPENDIX B: Lodging & Camping

We list Healdsburg first, including Dry Creek Valley and southern Alexander Valley lodgings. Northern and central Alexander Valley lodgings are listed under Cloverdale and Geyserville respectively.

HEALDSBURG, DRY CREEK VALLEY AND ALEXANDER VALLEY

HEALDSBURG

Belle de Jour Inn B&B
16276 Healdsburg Ave.
707-431-9777

Best Western Dry Creek Inn Motel
198 Dry Creek Road
707-433-0300

Calderwood Inn B&B
25 W. Grant
707-431-1110

Camellia Inn B&B
211 North Street
707-433-8182

Frampton House B&B
489 Powell Avenue
707-433-5084

George Alexander House B&B
423 Matheson
707-433-1358

Grapeleaf Inn B&B
539 Johnson
707-433-8140

Haydon Street Inn B&B
321 Haydon
707-433-5228

Healdsburg Inn on the Plaza B&B
110 Matheson
707-433-6991

Honor Mansion B&B
14891 Grove Street
707-433-4277

Madrona Manor B&B
1001 Westside Road
707-433-4231
A country inn and restaurant.

The River Rose
707-433-4305
Vacation Rentals.

Treavelodge
178 Dry Creek Road
707-433-0101

Villa Messina B&B
316 Burgundy Road
707-433-6655

GEYSERVILLE

Campbell Ranch Inn B&B
1475 Canyon Road
707-857-3476

Geyserville Inn & Deli
21714 Geyserville Ave.
707-857-4343

Hope-Merrill & Hope-Bosworth Houses B&B
21253 Geyserville Ave.
707-857-3356

CLOVERDALE

Abrams House Inn B&B
314 Main
707-894-2412

Vintage Towers B&B
302 N. Main
707-894-4535

Ye Olde Shelford House
29955 River Road
707-894- 5956

THE RUSSIAN RIVER: FORESTVILLE, GUERNEVILLE AND MONTE RIO

FORESTVILLE

The Farmhouse Inn and Restaurant
7871 River Road
707-887-3300

GUERNEVILLE

Applewood Inn & Restaurant B&B
13555 Highway 116
707-869-9093

Fifes: The Russian River's Foremost Gay Resort
16467 River Road
707-869-0656
Cabins and campsites, downtown.

Ridenhour Ranch House
12850 River Road
707-887-1033

MONTE RIO

North Woods Lodge & Resort
19455 Highway 116
707-865-1655

Village Inn
20822 River Boulevard
707-865-2304

SANTA ROSA

Vintners Inn
4350 Barnes Road
707-575-7350

THE COAST AND OCCIDENTAL

BODEGA

Bodega Estero B&B
17699 Highway 1
707-876-3300

BODEGA BAY

Bodega Bay Lodge Resort
103 Highway 1
707-875-3525

Bodega Harbor Inn
Hwy 1 and Bodega Ave.
707-875-3594

Chanslor Guest Ranch & Stables B&B
2660 Highway 1
707-875-2721

Inn at the Tides
800 Highway 1
707-875-2751

DUNCANS MILLS

Inn at Duncans Mills
25233 Steelhead Blvd.
707-865-1855

JENNER

Jenner Inn & Cottages
Highway 1
707-865-2377

River's End Inn
11051 Highway 1
707-865-2484

OCCIDENTAL

Inn at Occidental
3657 Church
707-874-1047

Negri's Occidental Lodge
3610 Bohemian Hwy
707-874-3623

Union Motel
3703 Main
707-874-3635

Winding Rose Inn
14985 Coleman Valley Rd
707-874-2680

FREESTONE

Green Apple Inn
520 Bohemian Highway
707-874-2526

VALLEY FORD

Inn at Valley Ford
14395 Highway 1
707-876-3182

POINT REYES STATION

For small hotels, country inns and cottages call 415-663-1872 or 800-539-1872.

Coastal Lodging of West Marin
415-663-1351

NORTH OF JENNER

Fort Ross Lodge
20705 Coast Highway 1
Fort Ross
707-847-3333

Timber Cove Inn
21780 Coast Highway 1
Timber Cove
707-847-3231

Salt Point Lodge
23255 Coast Highway 1
707-847-3234/
800-956-3437
Just south of Salt Point State Park

Timberhill Ranch
35755 Hauser Bridge Road
Cazadero
707-847-3258

Sea Ranch Lodge
60 Sea Walk Drive
P.O. Box 44, Sea Ranch
707-785-2371/
800-732-7262

CAMPING

Camping spots abound here in west Sonoma County and along the coast north to Gualala and south into western Marin County. Below we list our favorite spots along with some phone numbers to call for additional information. Reservations are recommended, and some sites may be closed during the winter season. For Sonoma Valley camping, refer to **Chapter 8.**

KOA Cloverdale Camping Resort
26460 River Road
707-894-3337

Campground at Lake Sonoma: 707-433-9483

California State Parks
General information: 916-653-6995
California State Parks Reservation Center:
800-444-7275

Austin Creek State Recreation Area
707-869-2015
Near Armstrong Redwoods
23 campsites, plus back-country sites.

Sonoma Coast State Beach
707-875-3483
These 16 miles of beaches, camping and picnic grounds extend from Bodega Head, to just north of Jenner at the mouth of the Russian River. Reservations are recommended.

Fort Ross State Park
Reef Campground: 707-847-3286
Salt Point State Park: 707-847-3221
These two state parks north of Jenner offer wonderful coastal camping. The first one is primitive and closes in winter, while the second has many units, full facilities and is open year round.

Sonoma County Regional Parks
General information: 707-527-2041

Stillwater Cove Regional Park: 707-847-3245
Gualala Point Regional Park: 707-785-2377
The County operates these two pleasant campgrounds along Highway 1 north of Fort Ross.

Westside and Doran Beach Regional Parks
Recorded message: 707-875-3540
The County operates these two pleasant campgrounds at Bodega Bay.

WESTERN MARIN COUNTY

Point Reyes National Seashore
415-663-1092
Backcountry camping only.

Samuel P. Taylor State Park
415-488-9897
Five miles east of Olema and fifteen miles west of San Rafael on Sir Frances Drake Boulevard, this park has 60 campsites in the cool redwoods along a lovely rushing stream. S. P. Taylor State Park offers a good place to camp while exploring the Point Reyes National Seashore and the Tomales Bay area. The state park also has a wonderfully shaded picnic area with great old-fashioned barbecues.

■ APPENDIX C: Resources

SUGGESTED READING

Access California Wine Country, Fourth edition, HarperCollins, 1998.

Doerper, John, *Coastal California*, Compass American Guides, Fodor's Travel Publications, 1998.

Doerper, John, *Wine Country,* Second edition, Compass American Guides, Fodor's Travel Publications, 1996.

Francisco, Cathleen, *Zinfandel; a current study*, Wine Appreciation Guild, 1998. Wine Key Publications, P.O. Box 14999, Santa Rosa, CA 95402.

Grissim, John, *West Marin Diary*, Floating Island Publications, 1991.

Halm, Meesha, and Dayna Macy, eds., *Savoring the Wine Country, Recipes from the Finest Restaurants of Northern California's Wine Region*, Collins Publishers, 1995.

Hinch, Stephen W., *Guide to the State Parks of the Sonoma Coast and Russian River*, Annadel Press, 1998.

Jordan, Michele Anna, *A Cook's Tour of Sonoma*, Addison Wesley Longman, 1990.

Katz, Andy, *A Portrait of Sonoma County*, Frequent Flyer Press, 1995 , out of print (o.p.).

Kroeber, A. L., *Handbook of the Indians of California*, Dover Publications, 1976.

Lorentzen, Bob, *The Hikers hip pocket Guide to Sonoma County*, Second edition, Bored Feet Press, 1995.

Lorentzen, Bob, and Richard Nichols, *Hiking the California Coastal Trail, Volume One: Oregon to Monterey*, Bored Feet Press, 1998.

Munro-Fraser, J.P., *History of Sonoma County, California, Illustrated*, Aley, Bowen & Co., 1880 (o.p.).

Newmann, Phyllis L., *Sonoma County Bike Trails*, Second edition, Penngrove Publications, 1996.

Roby, Norman S., and Charles E. Olken, *Connoisseur's Handbook of the Wines of California and the Pacific Northwest*, Fourth edition, Alfred A. Knopf, 1998.

Sterling, Joy, *A Cultivated Life: A Year in a California Vineyard*, Little, Brown & Co., 1994.

Sterling, Joy, *Vintage Feasting: A Vintner's Year of Fine Wines, Good Times, and gifts from Mother Nature*, Pocket Books, 1996.

Sterling, Joy, and Andy Katz, *Vineyard: A Year in the Life of California Wine Country*, Simon & Schuster, 1998.

Wilson, Simone, *Sonoma County: The River of Time, an Illustrated History*, Windsor Publications, 1990.

And, just for fun:

Brautigan, Richard, *Revenge of the Lawn*, Houghton Mifflin Co. 1995.

Brautigan, Richard, *Trout Fishing in America*, Houghton Mifflin Co. 1989.

Fisher, M. F. K., Anything!

Pukite, John, *A Field Guide to Cows: How to Identify and Appreciate America's 52 Breeds*, Viking Penguin, 1996.

Sarris, Greg, *Grand Avenue*, Viking Penguin, 1994.

Sarris, Greg, *Watermelon Nights*, Hyperion, 1998.

WEB GUIDE AND SUGGESTED BROWSING

The Internet provides easy access to a world of information. Almost every library has a computer station and the librarian will gladly help you navigate to those sites that will help you to plan your visit to Sonoma County.

We especially invite you to visit our web site,

www.sonomapicnic.com
The online wine country magazine.

Look for **sonoma picnic.com** to provide seasonal

updates to this book as well as in depth articles on the people, places, events and products of northern California. We strive to offer a focused catalog of related wine country books and maps as well as select picnic paraphernalia that you can order by mail.

California State Home Page: www.ca.gov

Cloverdale Home Page: www.cloverdale.net

Coastal Getaways: www.coastalgetaways.com
Information on five vacation rentals in the Point Reyes/Tomales Bay area of Marin County.

Counter Culture: www.counterculture.com
Online magazine, north coast news and views.

Golden Gate National Recreation Area: www.nps.gov/goga

How Far is it?: www.indo.com/distance
Determine the distance between any two places on the planet.

Jimtown Store: www.jimtown.com

KPIX TV Channel 5, San Francisco: www.kpix.com
News and weather.

Marin, Sonoma and Napa County Music Events: www.northbaymusic.com

National Park Service Park Net: www.nps.gov

Petaluma Area Chamber of Commerce: www.petaluma.org
History, maps, links and more.

Point Reyes Station Lodging: www.ptreyes.com

Russian River Chamber of Commerce: www.russianriver.com

Sonoma County Library: www.sonoma.lib.ca.us
You can access the catalog from the home page, but you must have a Telnet client that works with your browser. Or, try Telnet to sonoma.lib.ca.us.

Sonoma County Parks and Recreation: www.parks.sonoma.net

Sonoma County Transit:
server.berkeley.edu/transit/carriers/SCT ***
Bus schedules, news and system-wide map.

Sonoma County Wineries:
www.sonoma.com/sonoma/mwinerie.html

The Press Democrat: www.pressdemo.com
Sonoma County's outstanding daily paper.

Tribal Voice: www.tribal.com
Native American culture and history.

Union Hotel: www.unionhotel.com

THE WINERIES/WEST COUNTY:

Sonoma County Wineries Association:
www.sonomawine.com

Alderbrook Vineyards and Winery:
www.alderbrook.com

Belvedere Winery: www.belvedere-wines.com

Davis Bynum Winery: www.davisbynum.com

Dry Creek Vineyards:
www.dcv@drycreekvineyard.com

Iron Horse Vineyards:
www.ironhorsevineyards.com

Mill Creek Vineyards: www.mcvonline.com

Preston Vineyards: www.prestonvineyards.com

Quivira Vineyards: www.quivirawine.com

Simi Winery: www.simiwinery.com

THE WINERIES/EAST COUNTY:

Bartholomew Park Winery:
www.bartholomewparkwinery.com

Cline Cellars: www.clinecellars.com

Gundlach-Bundschu Winery:
www.gunbun.com

Ravenswood: www.ravenswood-wine.com

GUIDE TO LOCAL LIBRARIES

Sonoma County Central Library
3rd and E Streets
Downtown Santa Rosa
707-545-0831

Sonoma County History and Genealogy Annex
Located right next to the Central Library on 3rd Street, Santa Rosa
707-545-0831, Ext. 562

The History and Genealogy Annex is open from 10:00 a.m. to 6:00 p.m. Wed.–Sat. and is a wealth of information on all things local.

Healdsburg Regional Library
139 Piper Street
707-433-3772

Here you'll find the Sonoma County Wine Library, of particular interest. It houses a fascinating public collection on wineries and viticulture including a business and technical library for the local wine industry. Anyone interested in food and wine would enjoy some time in this great repository of wine history and cook's lore with its emphasis on Sonoma County.

Sonoma Valley Regional Library
755 W. Napa
Sonoma, CA
707-996-5217

◆

Many other communities have branch or local libraries. Consult the phone book.

GUIDE TO LOCAL NEWSPAPERS

Bodega Bay Navigator
707-875-3574

Published weekly on Thursdays and established in 1985, the Navigator *is a good source of community news, events and West County editorials. They also publish the* Coastal Navigator Guide *three times a year, available free throughout the area.*

Healdsburg Tribune
707-433-4451

Established in 1865, the Tribune *publishes weekly on Wednesdays with local news, views and events.*

Sonoma County Independent
707-527-1200

Sonoma County's free weekly arts and entertainment guide, published every Thursday and available throughout the county, also covers local issues, news and reviews.

Pacific Sun News Weekly
707-939-0234

Published weekly on Wednesdays since 1963, the Pacific Sun *is your guide to what's going on in the North Bay, with great club and music guides, event listings, and coverage of local issues.*

Press Democrat
707-546-2020 or
800-649-5056

Established in 1857, our award-winning morning daily is a first class source of local news, views and weather. They also have a great food and wine section every Wednesday, and local feature section on Thursdays.

Russian River Times
707-869-2010

Published twice a month since 1995, the Russian River Times *focuses on environmental, social justice, and health issues with River news, events and a nice tourist map in every issue.*

Sonoma Index-Tribune
707-938-2111

Sonoma Valley news and views since 1879.

Sonoma West Times and News
707-823-7845

First published in 1889 as the Sebastopol Times, *the* Sonoma West Times and News *comes out weekly on Wednesdays with West County news and views. They also publish an excellent quarterly guide called* Discovery *that is available free throughout the area.*

Point Reyes Light
415-663-8404

Western Marin County's award-winning weekly is published every Thursday.

■ APPENDIX D: Your Trip Plan

Here you will find phone numbers for emergency assistance. We hope you don't need them!

LOCAL EMERGENCY INFORMATION

Police or Fire, emergency only: call 911

For non-emergency police services:

> **Cloverdale:** 707-894-2150
>
> **Healdsburg:** 707-431-3377
>
> **Santa Rosa:** 707-528-5222
>
> **Sebastopol:** 707-829-4400
>
> **Sonoma County Sheriff:** 707-527-2511
>
> **Marin County Sheriff:** 415-499-7284
>
> **California State Highway Patrol, Santa Rosa Office:** 707-588-1400
>
> **United States Coast Guard, emergency only:** call 911
>
> **Search and Rescue Station at Bodega Bay:** 707-875-3596

VETERINARY EMERGENCY SERVICES

> **Petcare Emergency Hospital**
> 1370 Fulton Road, Santa Rosa
> 707-579-5900
> *24-hours*

If you're on a picnic and find orphaned or injured wildlife, contact:

> **Sonoma County Wildlife Rescue:** 707-526-9453 (Volunteer Staff Only)
>
> **Bird Rescue** 707-523-2473 (Volunteer Staff Only)

YOUR PERSONAL TRIP ITINERARY
AND PHONE NUMBERS:

_____

_____

_____

_____

_____

_____

_____

_____

_____

_____

_____

_____

_____

_____

_____

_____

_____

_____

_____

■ Index

■ About Bored Feet

We began Bored Feet Publications in 1986 to publish *The Hiker's hip pocket Guide to the Mendocino Coast*. Our company has grown by presenting the most accurate guidebooks for northern California. In 1999 we shortened our name to Bored Feet Press.

We love to hear your feedback about any of our publications. Also, if you'd like to receive updates on trails we cover in our publications, send us your name and address, specifying your counties of interest.

We also offer *FLEET FEET BOOKS*, our lightning fast mail/ phone order service offering books and maps about California and the West. Your purchases directly from Bored Feet support our independent publishing efforts to bring you more information about the gorgeous California coast. Thanks for your support!

If you would like more of our guides, please send check or money order or call for Visa/ Mastercard purchases. Please add $3 shipping for orders under $30, $5 over $30 ($5/7 for rush).

*THE ONLY COMPREHENSIVE GUIDES
TO CALIFORNIA'S NORTH COAST:*

Hiking the California Coastal Trail, Volume One: Oregon to Monterey	$18.00
Hiking the California Coastal Trail, Volume Two: Monterey to Mexico	18.00
Geologic Trips: San Francisco & the Bay Area	13.95
Great Day Hikes in & around the Napa Valley	12.00
Sonoma Picnic: A California Wine Country Travel Companion	12.00
Mendocino Coast Glove Box Guide, 2nd ed.	13.00
Mendocino Coast Bike Rides: Road & Trail Rides from Easy to Advanced	12.00
A Tour of Mendocino: 32 Historic Buildings	6.00
Hiker's hip pocket Guide to the Mendocino Coast, 3rd ed.	14.00
Hiker's hip pocket Guide to Sonoma County, 2nd ed.	15.00
Hiker's hip pocket Guide to the Humboldt Coast, 2nd ed.	14.00
Hiker's hip pocket Guide to the Mendocino Highlands (Yolla Bollys, etc.)	13.95
Boxed Gift Set: Mendocino Coast, Humboldt Coast, Sonoma County Hiker's Guides in silkscreened box	40.00
Yolla Bolly-Middle Eel Wilderness Trail Map	5.95
Trail of the Lost Coast Map	5.95

For shipping to a California address, please add 7.25 % sales tax.
PRICES SUBJECT TO CHANGE WITHOUT NOTICE.

BORED FEET PRESS
P.O. Box 1832
Mendocino, CA 95460
888-336-6199 · 707-964-6629
Fax: 707-964-5953
Email: boredfeet@mcn.org